Stuff Happens

David Hare, who was born in Sussex in 1947, is one of Britain's most internationally performed playwrights. Thirteen of his plays have been produced at Britain's National Theatre. A trilogy about the Church, the Law and the Labour Party – *Racing Demon*, *Murmuring Judges* and *The Absence of War* – was presented in repertory at the Olivier Theatre in 1993. Nine of his best-known plays, including *Plenty*, *The Secret Rapture*, *Skylight*, *The Blue Room*, *Amy's View*, *The Judas Kiss* and *Via Dolorosa* – in which he performed – have also been presented on Broadway.

by the same author

PLAYS ONE
(*Slag, Teeth 'n' Smiles, Knuckle, Licking Hitler, Plenty*)
PLAYS TWO
(*Fanshen, A Map of the World, Saigon,
The Bay at Nice, The Secret Rapture*)
THE GREAT EXHIBITION
RACING DEMON
MURMURING JUDGES
THE ABSENCE OF WAR
SKYLIGHT
AMY'S VIEW
THE JUDAS KISS
VIA DOLOROSA
MY ZINC BED
THE BREATH OF LIFE
THE PERMANENT WAY

adaptations
THE RULES OF THE GAME by Pirandello
THE LIFE OF GALILEO by Brecht
MOTHER COURAGE AND HER CHILDREN by Brecht
IVANOV by Chekhov
THE BLUE ROOM from *Reigen* by Schnitzler
PLATONOV by Chekhov
THE HOUSE OF BERNARDA ALBA by Lorca

screenplays for television
LICKING HITLER
DREAMS OF LEAVING
HEADING HOME

screenplays
COLLECTED SCREENPLAYS
(*Wetherby, Paris by Night, Strapless,
Heading Home, Dreams of Leaving*)
PLENTY
THE SECRET RAPTURE
THE HOURS

opera libretto
THE KNIFE

prose
ACTING UP
ASKING AROUND: BACKGROUND TO THE DAVID HARE TRILOGY
WRITING LEFT-HANDED

DAVID HARE

Stuff Happens

faber and faber

First published in 2004
by Faber and Faber Limited
3 Queen Square London WC1N 3AU
Published in the United States by Faber and Faber Inc.
an affiliate of Farrar, Straus and Giroux LLC, New York

Typeset by Country Setting, Kingsdown, Kent CT14 8ES
Printed in England by Mackays of Chatham plc, Chatham, Kent

David Hare is hereby identified as author
of this work in accordance with Section 77 of the
Copyright, Designs and Patents Act 1988

Extract from 'For the Time Being: A Christmas Oratorio'
from *Collected Poems* by W. H. Auden
© 1944 and renewed 1972, used by permission
of Random House Inc and Faber and Faber Ltd

All rights whatsoever in this work are strictly reserved.
Applications for permission for any use whatsoever including
performance rights must be made in advance, prior to any such
proposed use, to Casarotto Ramsay and Associates Ltd,
National House, 60–66 Wardour Street, London W1V 4ND.
No performance may be given unless a licence has first
been obtained

A CIP record for this book
is available from the British Library

ISBN 0–571–22606–X

4 6 8 10 9 7 5

In memoriam

Mary, Helen, Rory

Author's Note

Stuff Happens is a history play, which happens to centre on very recent history. The events within it have been authenticated from multiple sources, both private and public. What happened happened. Nothing in the narrative is knowingly untrue. Scenes of direct address quote people verbatim. When the doors close on the world's leaders and on their entourages, then I have used my imagination. This is surely a play, not a documentary, and driven, I hope, by its themes as much as by its characters and story.

I must thank all those people – some at the heart of these events, others to the side – who generously gave so much of their time and their knowledge to help my understanding. I owe much to Dr Christopher Turner, visiting scholar at Columbia University, who assisted me throughout. No bland formulation of thanks can do justice to the depth and detail of his research.

DH

Stuff Happens was first presented in the Olivier auditorium of the National Theatre on 1 September 2004, with the following cast:

George W. Bush Alex Jennings
Laura Bush Isla Blair
Dick Cheney Desmond Barrit
Colin Powell Joe Morton
Condoleezza Rice Adjoa Andoh
Donald Rumsfeld Dermot Crowley
George Tenet Philip Quast
Paul Wolfowitz Ian Gelder
Paul O'Neill Tim Donoghue
Michael Gerson Philip Quast
Mark Dayton Iain Mitchell
Dan Bartlett Alan Leith
John Negroponte Philip Quast
John McCain Tim Donoghue
Jessica Stern Isla Blair
David Kay Don Gallagher
Ari Fleischer Kevork Malikyan
Interviewer Sara Powell

Tony Blair Nicholas Farrell
Jack Straw Iain Mitchell
David Manning Angus Wright
Jonathan Powell Nick Sampson
Alastair Campbell Don Gallagher
Richard Dearlove Robert East
Philip Bassett Raad Rawi

Trevor McDonald Larrington Walker
Alan Simpson Ian Gelder
Jeremy Greenstock Alan Leith
Geoff Hoon Iain Mitchell
Robin Cook Don Gallagher

Jacques Chirac Ewan Hooper
Dominique de Villepin Nick Sampson
Maurice Gourdault-Montagne Philip Quast
Jean-David Levitte Tim Donoghue
Gérard Errera Raad Rawi

Saddam Hussein Raad Rawi
General Hassan Muhammad Amin Larrington Walker

Hans Blix Ewan Hooper
Kofi Annan Larrington Walker
Igor Ivanov Don Gallagher
Sergei Lavrov Kevork Malikyan
Mohammed ElBaradei Kevork Malikyan
Ricardo Lagos Raad Rawi
Yo-Yo Ma Iain Mitchell

Viewpoints
Angus Wright
Isla Blair
Raeda Ghazaleh
Iain Mitchell
Raad Rawi

Other parts played by members of the Company

Director Nicholas Hytner
Designer Christopher Oram
Lighting Designer Paul Anderson
Sound Designer Paul Groothuis
Associate Director Matt Wilde

STUFF HAPPENS

All of us have heard this term 'preventive war' since
the earliest days of Hitler. In this day and time . . .
I don't believe there is such a thing; and frankly
I wouldn't even listen to anyone seriously
that came in and talked about such a thing.

Dwight Eisenhower

It is useless to attempt to reason a man
out of a thing he was never reasoned into.

Jonathan Swift

Act One

ONE

As the audience arrive, the cast are already assembling onstage. Then the lights change and one of the Actors speaks.

An Actor The Inevitable is what will seem to happen to you purely by chance.

The Real is what will strike you as really absurd.

Unless you are certain you are dreaming, it is certainly a dream of your own.

Unless you exclaim – 'There must be some mistake' – you must be mistaken.

TWO

Another Actor steps forward.

An Actor Stuff. Happens. The response of Donald Rumsfeld, the American Secretary of Defense, when asked to comment on the widespread looting and pillage that followed the American conquest of Baghdad – Friday, April 11th 2003:

Journalist What's your response, sir? Mr Secretary, how do you respond to the news of looting and pillage in Baghdad?

Rumsfeld I've seen the pictures. I've seen those pictures. I could take pictures in any city in America. Think what's happened in our cities when we've had riots, and problems, and looting. Stuff happens! But in terms of what's going on in that country, it is a fundamental misunderstanding to see those images over and over and over again of some

3

boy walking out with a vase and say, 'Oh, my goodness, you didn't have a plan.' That's nonsense. They know what they're doing, and they're doing a terrific job. And it's untidy, and freedom's untidy, and free people are free to make mistakes and commit crimes and do bad things. They're also free to live their lives and do wonderful things, and that's what's going to happen here.

THREE

A line of civilians and soldiers head for a helicopter on a rooftop to evacuate Saigon.

An Actor So where to begin? To take the story back – April 25th 1975, the unforgettable event: the fall of Saigon. At last there are limits to American power.

Colin Powell steps forward.

Powell In Vietnam I learned a certain attitude, a certain distrust . . .

An Actor Major Colin Powell is pulled out of Vietnam six years earlier. By his own description, a serving soldier, schooled in obedience . . .

Powell The army is the most democratic institution in America.

An Actor November 1968: Powell is in a helicopter which falls to the ground, in his words, 'like an elevator with a snapped cable'.

Powell After Vietnam, many in my generation vowed that when our turn came to call the shots, we would not quietly acquiesce in half-hearted warfare for half-baked reasons. Politicians start wars; soldiers fight and die in them.

An Actor He is awarded the Legion of Merit and evolves what becomes known as the Powell doctrine:

Powell War should be the politics of last resort.

Donald Rumsfeld, peppy, in trifocals, steps forward.

An Actor Also in the seventies, Donald Rumsfeld, one-time champion wrestler, University of Chicago, is an assistant to Richard Nixon.

Rumsfeld I'd always worried about politicians who spent most of their time getting ready to *be* something as opposed to doing something. And I questioned whether that was a great way to live a life, getting ready as opposed to doing.

An Actor One friend says of Rumsfeld:

Rumsfeld's First Friend When you play squash with him, you are lucky not to have your head taken off with his racquet. The court is a finite place. If you are between him and the wall, Rumsfeld always fires away.

An Actor A second friend says:

Rumsfeld's Second Friend In locker-room terms, Don is a towel-snapper.

Dick Cheney, rock-hard, bland, steps forward.

An Actor In the same White House, jostling for position, is the young Dick Cheney, who has achieved a total of five student deferments in order to avoid being drafted to Vietnam.

Cheney I had other priorities in the sixties than military service.

An Actor Cheney proves himself willing to take on responsibilities others shirk.

Cheney Memo from Dick Cheney, October 12th 1974. We will be unable in the short term to fix the drainage problem in the sink in the first-floor bathroom. The White House plumbing is very old and we have had the

General Services Administration working for some time to figure out how to improve this problem.

An Actor When Cheney moves into elected politics, he is already uncompromising.

Cheney I never met a weapons system I didn't vote for.

Condoleezza Rice, splendid, always alone, steps forward.

An Actor At the same time, at Stanford University, a minister's daughter from Birmingham, Alabama, Condoleezza Rice, is choosing between a professional music career or a life in academia studying the Soviet bloc.

Rice Like most Americans I listened with some scepticism to the Cold War claim that America was a 'beacon of democracy'. My ancestors were property – a fraction of a man. Women were not included in those immortal constitutional phrases concerning the right of the people 'in the course of human events' to choose who would rule.

An Actor When asked by Yo-Yo Ma:

Yo-Yo Ma Who is your favourite composer?

Rice Brahms.

Yo-Yo Ma Why? Why Brahms?

Rice He's passionate without being sentimental.

Yo-Yo Ma Do you think it's also this irresolution in Brahms, the tension that is never resolved?

An Actor In her office Rice keeps two mirrors, so she can see her back as well as her front.

Paul Wolfowitz, suited, intent, steps forward.

At another university, a Yale professor, Paul Wolfowitz, spends the nineteen seventies chewing over the implications of the involvement in Vietnam which he describes as:

Wolfowitz An over-expenditure of American power.

An Actor An ex-maths whiz, Wolfowitz is in love with the idea of national greatness.

Wolfowitz I focus on geo-strategic issues. I consider myself conceptual. I am willing to re-examine entire precepts of US foreign policy.

An Actor One colleague remarks:

Colleague The word 'hawk' doesn't do Wolfowitz justice. What about velociraptor?

Tony Blair, direct, vigorous, steps forward.

An Actor At the same time, in England, a fledgling lawyer, just down from Oxford, is recovering from the sudden, premature death of his mother and beginning a relationship with another lawyer in the same chambers.

Blair It was late before I had any politics at all.

An Actor A friend remarks:

Blair's Friend You'd be at a party and you'd turn round and find that Tony had gone. He'd slipped away a couple of hours before. You'd find he was getting up at five o'clock to finish an essay.

An Actor Fired up by an original mix of theology and social duty, Blair will become Britain's youngest Labour MP.

Blair I particularly resent the assumption that if you find Neanderthal elements in the Labour Party, you have found the real party.

An Actor He refuses to list his early positions in *Who's Who*.

Blair I do not regard being a Shadow Cabinet front-bench spokesman as a real job. I did not join the Labour Party to join a party of protest. I joined it as a party of government and I will make sure that it is a party of government.

Kofi Annan, gentle, imposing, steps forward.

An Actor In the nineteen seventies, Kofi Annan, the son of a Fanti tribal chief, whose name means –

Annan Born on a Friday.

An Actor – is working as Managing Director of the Ghanaian Tourist Development Company, operating duty-free shops at the Kotoka International Airport, Accra.

Annan I wanted to make a contribution to Ghana but I found myself constantly fighting the military, so I went back to the UN.

An Actor His keen sense of the possible, Annan says, comes from watching the Ghanaian struggle for independence.

Annan I feel profoundly African, my roots are deeply African.

An Actor Most people are drawn to him by the timbre of voice, like an amplified whisper:

Annan Imagine a pool of fresh, clear water. Beyond the pool, there are some steps, and you are going down the steps . . .

Hans Blix, with an air of mild amusement, steps forward.

An Actor And finally, in Sweden, a graduate of Uppsala university, Hans Blix, is finding his way in Liberal Party politics.

Blix I was an amateur actor when I was a student. Theatre teaches you the value of collaboration, of getting on with other people. As well, of course, as being damned enjoyable.

An Actor Blix is already developing an attitude to life which Colin Powell will one day find praiseworthy.

Powell He's as reliable as a Volvo.

Blix Being aware that one of Powell's favourite hobbies is working on Volvo engines, I took this as praise.

The eight central characters step forward.

An Actor These are the actors, these are the men and women who will play parts in a defining drama of the new century. And at their head is a snappish young man, seeking his fortune in the oil-rich Permian Basin of West Texas, who will, one day, like forty-six per cent of his fellow Americans, say he has been born again.

Bush steps among them.

Bush My faith frees me. Frees me to put the problem of the moment in proper perspective. Frees me to make decisions which others might not like. Frees me to enjoy life and not worry about what comes next.

You know I had a drinking problem. Right now I should be in a bar in Texas, not in the Oval Office. There is only one reason I am in the Oval Office and not a bar. I found God. I am here because of the power of prayer.

An Actor The elder son of a Kennebunkport dynasty, George W. Bush is considered the joke of the family, beside his more favoured brother Jeb. He only enters politics at the age of forty-seven.

Bush I could not be governor if I did not believe in a divine plan which supersedes all human plans.

An Actor When he runs for President, he observes:

Bush I feel like God wants me to run for President. I can't explain it, but I sense my country is going to need me. Something is going to happen and at that time my country is going to need me. I know it won't be easy, on me or on my family, but God wants me to do it.

An Actor His Deputy Under-Secretary for Defense will observe:

Lt General Why is this man in the White House? The majority of Americans did not vote for him. Why is he there? And I tell you this morning that he's in the White House because God put him there for a time such as this.

An Actor Bush will lose the popular vote by a margin of 539,898. Upon his taking up office, he will observe:

Bush I'm the commander – see, I don't need to explain. I don't need to explain why I say things. That's the interesting thing about being the President. Maybe somebody needs to explain to me why they say something. But I don't feel like I owe anybody an explanation.

FOUR

Bush, fastidiously punctual, is already in place, sitting alone at the head of a torpedo-shaped table.

An Actor The new administration hits the ground running. Ten days after his inauguration, on January 30th 2001, President Bush presides at a meeting of the National Security Council for the first time.

> *Bush is joined by a group including Powell, Cheney, Rumsfeld, Tenet, Rice, O'Neill and a rank of generals. Behind, everyone has deputies.*

Bush I believe we all have a piece of paper. This first meeting, we take the Middle East. Condi?

Rice If I can express what the President is feeling, we wish to start by sharply differentiating ourselves from the previous administration. President Clinton's attempts to broker a deal between the Israelis and the Palestinians not only took up a huge amount of time, they also left this country looking weak. The President's view is that the time has come to tilt back towards Israel. You'll say, sir, if I misrepresent you?

Bush says nothing.

Cheney Please continue.

Rice The President feels that the fortunes of the region need to be decided by the players themselves. This present administration isn't going to take on problems it knows it can't solve.

Bush Anybody here met Sharon?

Colin Powell lifts a hand.

Powell I've met him. I know him.

Bush I want to take the guy at face value. With Sharon we have this policy: we don't go by past reputation.

Rice The President feels very strongly that we're a new administration. The relationship should be judged not by how it's been in the past but how it proceeds.

Bush Sharon flew me in a helicopter over the Palestinian camps. Looked real bad down there.

There is a short silence.

I think this is one we want to get out of.

There is another short silence.

Rice Any comments?

Powell If I may, sir.

They all look at Powell.

I don't need to give a lecture about the intensity of feelings in the Middle East. This is a problem with deep historical roots. We're not prisoners of history, but on the other hand we can't pretend history never happened.

Rumsfeld What's your point?

Powell On the ground there's a conflict. Left to himself, Sharon's instincts are always to rack up that conflict – and always by military means. If we disengage, the risk is, we unleash Sharon. The consequences of that will be dire for the Palestinians.

Bush Well, maybe that's what's needed. Maybe that's the best way to get things back in balance.

There's a silence.

You know, sometimes, in my experience, a real show of strength by just one side can clarify things. It can make things really clear.

Powell looks at him a moment.

Now let's move on. Iraq.

O'Neill Iraq?

An Actor Paul O'Neill. Secretary of the Treasury.

O'Neill Iraq?

But Tenet is already unfurling a large aerial photograph onto the table.

Rice Yeah, that's right, we're going to have a briefing. The CIA Director's going to brief us, get us up to speed on the latest intelligence.

An Actor George Tenet. Director, CIA.

Tenet I'm going to ask you all to take a look at this photograph.

Rice The real danger to the region . . .

Tenet If we can all study this photograph . . .

Rice Correctly analysed, when you correctly analyse the region, the real threat is destabilisation.

Tenet Here's the photograph.

Rice And where's that going to come from? It's going to come from Saddam Hussein.

Tenet I hope everyone can see the photograph.

Rice I think we ought to keep our eye on that.

Tenet There's the railroad, there are the tracks . . . look over here and you'll see the trucks coming in . . .

Rumsfeld There're the trucks . . .

Tenet There's the water-cooler. This was taken by surveillance planes, so the quality is kind of grainy . . .

Cheney signals to military deputies sitting behind.

Cheney Everyone come see this. You don't want to miss this.

Rumsfeld It's grainy, but you can see . . .

Tenet This looks to us . . .

Rumsfeld You can see clearly . . .

Tenet I think the CIA believes . . .

Rumsfeld Even I can see, and I'm nearly seventy . . .

Tenet This might well be a plant which produces either chemical or biological materials for weapons manufacture.

Everyone is crowded round the photograph.

Bush Yeah. Yeah.

Rice Everyone see?

O'Neill I can see. But – I'm asking, I'm just asking: I've seen an awful lot of factories round the world that look an awful lot like this. What's the evidence, what's the evidence of what this factory's producing?

Tenet Well, it's rhythm.

O'Neill Rhythm?

Tenet Rhythm of shipment. Round the clock. In and out of the plant. Trucks coming and going all night. The rhythm is consistent. Look, let's be clear: I'm not saying it is, I'm not saying they are . . .

Rumsfeld You're not saying it's not.

Tenet I'm not.

Rumsfeld He's not saying anything.

Tenet Not quite.

Rumsfeld He's from the CIA.

They all laugh.

Tenet There is no confirming intelligence, no, that they are definitely producing chemical or biological weapons. I am not claiming that. I'm saying, 'Look at the photo – look at it – and what you will see is a factory clearly consistent.' And if they were producing such weapons – *if* – if they were, if such weapons were being produced, then this – seen here – would be the kind of factory, this looks just like the factory from which such weapons would come.

There is a silence.

Bush We need to know more about this. We need to know more about the weapons.

FIVE

An angry British Journalist appears.

Journalist The absurdity of it. The absurdity and the irrelevance. The idea of discussing even . . . a historical event, an invasion already more than a year old. A country groaning under a dictator, its people oppressed, liberated at last from a twenty-five year tyranny – and freed. Free on the streets, and free one day to vote.

How obscene it is, how decadent, to give your attention not to the now, not to the liberation, not to the people freed, but to the relentless archaic discussion of the *manner* of the liberation. Was it lawful? Was it not? How was it done? What were the details of its doing? Whose views were overridden? Whose views condoned?

Do I like the people who did it? Are they my kind of people? Hey – are they stupider than me?

How spoiled, how indulged we are to discuss the manner – oh yes, we discuss the manner, late into the night, candles guttering, our faces sweating, reddening with wine and hatred – but the act itself – the thing done – the splendid thing done – freedom given to people who were not free – this thing is ignored, preferring as we do to fight among ourselves – our own disputes, our own resentment of each other elevated way above the needs of the victims. 'I trust Blair/I don't.' 'I like Bush/I don't.' 'Bush is stupid/Bush is clever.' This obsession with our-selves! How Western we are. From what height of luxury and excess we look down to condemn the exact style in which even a little was given to those who had nothing.

Saddam Hussein attacked every one of his neighbours except Jordan. Imagine, if you will, if you are able, a dictator in Europe, murdering his own people, attacking his neighbours, killing half a million people for no other offence but proximity. Do you really then imagine, hand on heart, that the finer feelings of the international community, the exact procedures of the United Nations would need to be tested, would the finer points of sovereignty detain us, before we rose, as a single force, to overthrow the offender? Would we ask, faced with the bodies, faced with the gas, faced with the ditches and the murders, would we really stop to say, 'Can we do this?' What is the word, then, for those of us in the West who apply one standard to ourselves, and another to others? What is the word for those who claim to love democracy and yet who will not fight to extend democracy to Arabs as well?

A people hitherto suffering now suffer less. This is the story. No other story obtains.

SIX

Bush sits on a low chair reading to children in a kindergarten.

An Actor September 11th 2001. At 8.46 a.m. American Airlines Flight 11 from Boston, hijacked by suicide bombers, crashes into the North Tower of the World Trade Center in New York. Seventeen minutes later, United Airlines Flight 175, also from Boston, crashes into the South.

An aide leans in to Bush's ear.

An Actor In Sarasota, Florida, the President makes a brief statement.

Bush The full resources of the federal government will be employed to investigate and find those folks who committed this act. Terrorism against our nation will not stand.

An Actor At 9.39 a.m., a third plane, American Airlines Flight 77, smashes into the Pentagon. A fourth, United

Airlines Flight 93, aimed at the White House, is diverted by the bravery of its passengers and also crashes. President Bush is flown to Barksdale Air Force Base in Louisiana, where he records a statement to be broadcast only when he is once again airborne.

Bush Make no mistake. The United States will hunt down and punish those responsible for these cowardly acts. Freedom itself was attacked this morning by a faceless coward. And freedom will be defended.

An Actor The President is moved to an underground bunker at Strategic Command, Offutt Air Base, Nebraska. At his own insistence, he is flown back to the White House, whence he broadcasts live to the nation at 8.30 p.m.

Bush We will make no distinction between the terrorists who committed these acts and those who harbour them. None of us will forget this day. Yet we go forward to defend freedom and all that is good and just in our world.

Exhausted staff gather to hear the President.

An Actor He then addresses his team in the Presidential Emergency Operations Center:

Bush I want you all to understand that we are at war, and we will stay at war until this is done. Nothing else matters. Everything is available for the pursuit of this war. Any barriers in your way, they're gone. Any money you need, you have it. This is our only agenda.

The staff dissolve.

An Actor On Iraqi television a spokesman for Saddam Hussein declares:

Iraqi Spokesman The massive explosions in the centres of power are a painful slap in the face of US politicians to stop their illegitimate hegemony and attempts to impose custodianship on peoples. The American cowboy is reaping the fruits of his crimes against humanity.

An Actor In England Tony Blair declares:

Blair This is not a battle between the United States of America and terrorism, but between the free and democratic world and terrorism.

An Actor The French newspaper *Le Monde* has a headline:

Le Monde We are all Americans now.

An Actor By nightfall, 2,948 people of ninety-one different nationalities are dead. Four days later, on September 15th, the President assembles his War Cabinet for a weekend at Camp David.

SEVEN

The War Cabinet – including Bush, Rice, Wolfowitz, Powell, O'Neill, Tenet, Cheney and Rumsfeld, now in casual clothes – assembles in a wood-panelled room at Camp David.

Bush We'll begin this meeting as we always do.

Everyone closes their eyes.

Oh God, who gives everything and knows everything, direct our thoughts, give our thoughts direction, make us wise, give us wisdom, that we may surely do good. In thy name.

All Amen.

Everyone resettles.

Bush I'm going to be asking everyone to make reports, I'm going to be asking everyone to talk informally, so we can look at options, different ways of going . . .

O'Neill I'm proud to be able to say: the New York Stock Exchange is indeed going to be open on Monday.

Bush I've said that's important.

O'Neill We're sending out a signal, and the signal is: business as usual.

An Actor As the day went on, the War Cabinet began to hear of a global network of terror in over fifty countries, of which Osama bin Laden and Al Qaeda were only one part . . .

Tenet gets up and hands out identical intelligence dossiers to everyone.

Tenet Within this dossier you'll find up-to-date information of terror organisations. The plan inside focuses on expanded powers for the CIA. We're asking for a kind of global charge – the right to attack any aspect of a terrorist network without specific case-by-case clearance from the President.

Bush This is a war. This is a war on terror.

Tenet The most important objective for us is to concentrate our efforts providing money and resources for the Northern Alliance within Afghanistan, to make sure that if we go in, we can energise support, we can make sure there are people ready to take over the running of the country when the Taliban falls.

Bush I tell you how I see Afghanistan. I see it as a 'demonstration model'.

Rice Speaking with the President, what the President's been saying to me is that Afghanistan can be used as a kind of example . . .

Bush That's what it is.

Rice That's right.

Bush An example.

Rice That's right.

Bush A model, it's a kind of model . . .

Rice Afghanistan is a kind of demonstration model, so that other countries can look and say, 'Oh I see. That's what happens . . .'

Bush 'I see . . .'

Rice 'That's what happens.'

O'Neill What other countries d'you have in mind?

Bush Iran.

O'Neill OK.

Bush For example.

There's a silence.

Rice We want to send a message to countries which are considering actions hostile to the United States.

Bush Wolfie . . .

Wolfowitz Well, I want to talk about another country, it's another country in the Middle East, let's talk about that category of countries which is considering actions hostile to the United States. And if you take a good look at that category then I think there's one egregious member. It's been in violation of United Nations resolutions for over ten years.

Rumsfeld I sent a memo, if you remember, Mr President, in January, before this happened, I sent a memo with a list of countries who I considered were eager to exploit any lapses in US capability. China, North Korea, Russia, Iran. My conclusion was we should take any actions necessary to dissuade nations from challenging American interests. Top of that list was Iraq.

Bush nods.

Wolfowitz We're talking a corrupt dictatorship, run by a man who oppresses his own people and thumbs his nose at American power. We're talking about going in and establishing democracy. This is a country which is now very brittle. It will break very easily. It's sitting there, waiting to fall. This is something we can do with very little effort. For a minimum expenditure of effort, we can get maximum result. Take out Saddam and we blow fresh air into the Middle East.

Rumsfeld I mean, Jumping Jiminy, look at it strategically . . .

Wolfowitz That's it . . .

Rumsfeld Look at it: Afghanistan's a big country, but what are we going to bomb? Tommy Franks says there are only three dozen targets. Three dozen! Have you looked at Afghanistan? Terracotta pots and straw roofs! It isn't easy. You can do it . . .

Wolfowitz Oh sure, you can do it . . .

Rumsfeld We'll do it. Anything we're asked to do, we'll do. But it's hard. The only thing you can say for it, at least it isn't the Balkans. We're not like Clinton . . .

Cheney We're not . . .

Bush Hell, we're not . . .

Rumsfeld It's not the Balkans . . .

Cheney If there's one thing we can agree on . . .

Rumsfeld Wasting time in a place full of ethnic hatreds. Pounding sand. But that doesn't mean it's easy. It isn't easy.

Wolfowitz Attacking Afghanistan will be uncertain. I'm not saying we won't succeed . . .

Rumsfeld We'll succeed.

Wolfowitz Yeah. But what I'm concerned about is, OK, there we are in maybe six months' time with a hundred thousand American soldiers –

Rumsfeld Don't say 'bogged down' . . .

Wolfowitz All right, let's say 'snarled up' – a hundred thousand American soldiers snarled up! OK? In mountain fighting. What message does that send? What example? Whereas, look . . . Iraq's a country we know. We've been there. And more important – talking about sending messages – I'd say there's a good percentage chance Saddam Hussein was directly involved in the attacks on the World Trade Center.

Bush Reckon that, Paul. What percentage?

Wolfowitz Ten to fifty. That's where I'd put it. A ten to fifty per cent chance.

Everyone is thoughtful.

Rice Mr President, Afghanistan is a country – this is a place with a history. It was nemesis for the British in the nineteenth century. It was nemesis for the Russians in the twentieth. All I'm concerned is it isn't our turn in the twenty-first.

Nobody says anything.

Wolfowitz That's what's good about Iraq. It's do-able.

The Cabinet breaks up and goes for soup and sandwiches.

An Actor They stopped for lunch.

Bush There's chicken noodle soup. Home-made.

Wolfowitz Wonderful . . .

O'Neill Smells good.

Rumsfeld I could eat a baby through the bars of a cot.

Bush We bake our own bread here. They bake the bread.

O'Neill Kind of thing your mother served you.

Bush Not my mother. Not my mother at all. She never cooked. That woman had frostbite on her fingers. Everything out of the freezer.

Everyone laughs.

It's good to be eating this kind of food. It's comfort food. It's good to be eating it now.

An Actor Then in the afternoon they went back to it.

The meeting resumes.

Rumsfeld I'd like to move on to a subject I think important. It's not a subject. It's an approach. There's a mistake they made during the first Gulf War. They were too specific. Remember? They talked all the time about Saddam Hussein. That had an effect. It elevated the guy. Now he's still there and everyone says, 'Hey – they screwed up.' We want to avoid that mistake.

Bush Huh.

Rumsfeld Look, sir, understand – not to pre-empt any decision . . .

Bush raises a hand in permission.

But I think we're all beginning to feel a consensus. OK, we accept what we have to do first. We have to go after Al Qaeda and get its leader. We want to take out Osama bin Laden, we want to take out Mohammad Omar, we want to isolate them in their camps and destroy them. But I'm not sure that's the rhetoric we should be using. Because I'm just pointing out – if we set targets, if we make targets, specific targets, if we make objectives and then we don't hit them – (*Rumsfeld waits a moment.*) If we turn this guy into some kind of monster – this great monster Osama bin Laden – I mean, I'm saying I don't think the President should even mention him.

Bush Huh.

Rumsfeld I liked what you said earlier, sir. A war on terror. That's good. That's vague.

Cheney It's good.

Rumsfeld That way we can do anything.

There's a short silence.

An Actor By nightfall they were tired. Nobody summed up. But, towards the end:

Powell We've heard a lot of plans . . .

Bush Colin.

Powell We've heard a lot of different ideas. And that's OK. But one thing I'd say: we have to be take care. Step by step. If we go into Afghanistan, we're going to need Pakistan. And that's going to be a risk for Musharraf.

Bush Is he ready to take that risk?

Powell I believe he is, sir. The guy is genuine. He wants a secular, Westernised country. That's what Musharraf wants and he's willing to risk a lot to get it. But there are also dangers for us. Afghanistan is already a mess. Pakistan sides with us and the danger is that country's destabilised as well. Suddenly the whole region's on fire. The point I'm making: this exercise is going to need patience. How we do things is going to be just as important as what we do. My job will be to assemble an international coalition. A coalition of countries who want to show their support for us and for the values we share in common. Here, today, we can talk among ourselves, we can say, 'Oh let's go do Iraq, or hey, it's time to fix Iran . . .' But. Since Tuesday we have the support of the whole world. People don't want to go for one thing, and then find they've signed up for another. Nobody likes bait and switch. Who we go against is going to decide who goes with us.

Bush Sure. (*Bush nods.*) You know, Colin, finally this is a war on terror. And at some point we may be the only ones left. That's fine with me.

There's a silence. Then they break up.

An Actor The meeting broke up.

Bush Here they come . . .

Rumsfeld Good evening, ladies.

In come the wives – Laura Bush, Joyce Rumsfeld, Nancy O'Neill, etc.

An Actor Their wives joined them and they all had supper.

Tenet What have we got tonight?

Laura Fried chicken, corn-bread, mashed potatoes and gravy.

Rumsfeld Hey, OK. I'll have the fried chicken, the corn-bread, the mashed potatoes and the gravy.

Everyone laughs.

An Actor An artist had made a jigsaw of the White House with the Bushes standing in front of it. So, after dinner, the President sat with his wife and they worked quietly, putting the little bits of their family and their house together.

Bush sits with Laura assembling the jigsaw.

Bush That looks like you, Laura. That looks like a bit of you, sweetheart.

Laura I'll work on the columns, you work on the people.

An Actor Nobody knew what to do, but nobody wanted to leave.

Everyone is now sitting around, relaxed.

Rice Anyone want to go bowling?

Bush I'm not bowling tonight, no way. Oh no.

Laura Anyone know any hymns?

Rice Yeah. Yeah. I know some hymns.

The room falls silent. Rice begins to sing.

Amazing grace! How sweet the sound
That saved a wretch like me!
I once was lost, but now am found;
Was blind, but now I see.

Everyone joins in.

Through many dangers, toils and snares
I have already come;
'Tis grace hath brought me safe thus far,
And grace will lead me home.

EIGHT

Congress. Legislators greet the arrival of Bush, accompanied by Tony Blair.

An Actor On September 17th the President signs an executive order authorising attacks on Afghanistan. Three days later he addresses Congress:

Bush Every nation, in every region, now has a decision to make. Either you are with us or you are with the terrorists.

An Actor In the balcony above him is the British Prime Minister. At one point Bush looks up:

Bush Thank you for coming, friend.

Blair receives a standing ovation in Congress, then moves to a lectern in Brighton.

An Actor Soon after, back in England, Blair addresses the Labour Party conference:

Blair The state of Africa is a scar on the conscience of the world. But if the world as a community focused on it, we could heal it. And if we don't, it will become deeper and angrier. This is the moment to tackle problems from the slums of Gaza to the mountain ranges of Afghanistan. This is a moment to seize. The kaleidoscope has been shaken. The pieces are in flux. Soon they will settle again. Before they do, let us reorder this world around us.

An Actor On October 7th the US and Britain begin air and missile strikes against thirty-one Al Qaeda and Taliban targets.

Rumsfeld appears for a press conference, flanked by generals.

Rumsfeld The campaign's going well, couldn't be going better. After two days we are now able to carry out strikes more or less round the clock and we've been hitting eighty-five per cent of our targets. Some of the targets we hit need to be re-hit.

Laughter.

Journalist What are you saying, Mr Secretary? Are you saying you're running out of targets?

Rumsfeld We're not running out of targets. Afghanistan is.

More laughter.

You know, if you try to quantify what we're doing today in terms of previous conventional wars, you're making a huge mistake. That is 'old think' and that will not help you analyse what we're doing. It's a different kind of conflict.

The press conference becomes a swanky Washington dinner.

An Actor One month later, Rumsfeld is thunderously received when he addresses a black-tie dinner of defence contractors:

Rumsfeld The coalition will not determine the mission. The mission will determine the coalition. We will not stop for Ramadan. We will not stop for winter. And after the Taliban and Al Qaeda we'll get after the rest.

Jack Straw steps forward.

An Actor In Europe, the British Foreign Secretary, Jack Straw, is regularly put forward to control the impact of statements from Rumsfeld and the Pentagon:

Straw There are always statements coming out of Washington. Washington is a very large place. But this military coalition is about action in respect of military and terrorist targets in Afghanistan.

An Actor On November 13th, after five years under an extreme religious regime, the Northern Alliance enter and liberate the capital, Kabul.

Bush is in the Oval Office, Cheney and Rice with him, listening to the call on speakerphone. Blair, David Manning, Jonathan Powell, and Alastair Campbell are in Blair's den in Downing Street.

Bush Tony. Hi. Good to hear you.

Blair Hello.

Bush You've heard the good news? You've been hearing the good news?

Blair Yes. It's all very good, I agree. It's mostly good. But there's one issue I need to raise.

There's a silence. Bush looks straight ahead.

Bush Raise your issue.

Blair It's this. As you know, British special forces have been working on the Pakistani border, around Tora Bora . . .

Bush I know that.

Blair Seeking out bin Laden. I'm sure you've also been told that just a few days ago, we found him. We tracked him.

Bush I got those reports.

Blair The point is this: when we found him, our special forces received a request from the US special forces. We were ordered to pull out.

There's another silence. Rice looks to Cheney.

Now I don't know where that particular order came from . . .

Bush It's an operational decision . . .

Blair Of course . . .

Bush It's not taken at this level.

Blair No. I accept that. But I also have great respect for my military . . .

Bush I respect my military.

Blair That's the reason I'm calling. As of now, I've got some angry generals. A decision was made – George, I'm not saying you made it, I'm sure it wasn't you – whoever –

Blair is offering Bush the chance to speak, but he says nothing.

In fact, I don't know if you even know who took it – who took that decision –

Blair waits again. Bush looks to Cheney, who shakes his head very slightly.

Bush Go on.

Blair We're both – you and I both – look, it's clear – capturing bin Laden has tremendous significance . . .

Bush That could be.

Blair Tremendous impact. And in the world as it is, the British army capturing him would not ring the same bells as if you had caught him. I accept that.

There is another silence. Both groups on either side of the Atlantic are still.

I don't want to labour this.

Bush You're not labouring it, Tony. You're making a point. We don't ever not hear you.

Blair looks to Manning, who rolls his eyes.

Blair As of December 11th, bin Laden has gone off the map. Intelligence has lost him. In the time between when we were ordered to withdraw and you going in, bin Laden escaped.

Bush Yes.

There is silence. Bush nods slightly.

Thank you for raising that, Tony. What other matters are you thinking to raise?

The two camps dissolve.

An Actor Not long after, the President remarks:

Bush Our objective is more than bin Laden. I just don't spend that much time on him, to be honest. Focusing on one person indicates to me that people don't understand the scope of this mission. Terror is bigger than one man.

An Actor By the end of 2001, the US will have spent $6.46 billion on the bombing of Afghanistan.

Bush takes Rumsfeld's arm and leads him from a
corridor into a small office.

Bush Donald, I need to see you alone.

An Actor On November 21st 2001, George Bush leads
Donald Rumsfeld into an empty office next to the
Situation Room.

Bush Donald, I know you're doing a worldwide review.
I've been thinking: it could provide a very good cover.

Rumsfeld What sort of cover?

Bush What kind of war plan do you have for Iraq? How
do you feel about the war plan for Iraq? Let's get started
on this. Get Tommy Franks looking at it.

An Actor It is seventy-two days after September 11th.

Bush And Donald – don't tell anyone else.

NINE

A New Labour Politician appears. She is direct, to the
point.

Politician We know the world. We know how the world
is. Something is decided. Something has to be done. If
each of us waited for the perfect circumstances, nothing
would ever be achieved.

At a certain moment, Dick Cheney, Donald Rumsfeld,
Paul Wolfowitz – three different men, but all wishing the
world better, wishing the world changed – prompt the
President. 'Do it now. If it is not done now, it will never
be done.'

They saw an opening, and in they went.

I understand the feelings of those who wish things
might have been done differently. In a different way. At
a different time. We may all wish that. But who said

'Politics is the art of the possible'? You do what you can. Because in politics, in life, one thing is certain: there will always be reasons not to act.

I can't put my hand on my heart and say things are going to work out in Iraq. How do I know? How can anyone say that? We walk backwards into the future. A dictator was removed. Reasons were offered for that removal which have proved, with hindsight, not to be justified. Weapons believed to exist turned out not to exist. A flawless military victory was compromised by sloppy Pentagon planning for peace. Practices evolved on the ground which everyone admits were unworthy of a great cause. But the action itself remains pure.

Do you know, do you have any idea how rare it is, for even one moment in the disorderly unfolding of events, to achieve purpose?

And now? Now we can only wait.

TEN

A team of sweating speech-writers circle, reading out explosive rhetorical sections of the forthcoming speech. Michael Gerson is in charge.

An Actor January 29th 2002: George Bush uses his State of the Union address to rack up the rhetoric. The President's chief speech-writer, Michael Gerson, calls this:

Gerson A plastic, teachable moment.

An Actor Gerson instructs his team:

Gerson Make the best case for war in Iraq. But leave exit ramps.

Bush enters a cheering Congress and shakes eager hands.

An Actor Dick Cheney sits directly behind as the President reads the result:

Bush Iraq continues to flaunt its hostility towards America and to support terror. States like these, and their terrorist allies, constitute an axis of evil, arming to threaten the peace of the world. By seeking weapons of mass destruction, these regimes pose a grave and growing danger.

All nations should know: America will do what is necessary to ensure our nation's security. I will not wait on events, while dangers gather. I will not stand by as peril draws closer and closer.

History has called America and our allies to action. Steadfast in our purpose, we now press on. We have known freedom's price. We have shown freedom's power. And in this great conflict, my fellow Americans, we will see freedom's victory.

An Actor Paul Wolfowitz recalls:

Wolfowitz It was when I heard that speech I thought: the President really gets it.

An Actor The President himself says of the phrase 'axis of evil':

Bush It just kind of resonates.

An Actor At once, alarm bells start to go off in European capitals. The French Foreign Minister calls the speech:

French Foreign Minister Simplistic.

An Actor The German Foreign Minister warns:

German Foreign Minister Alliance partners are not satellites.

An Actor A British Foreign Office official observes:

Foreign Office Official We all smiled at the jejune language. It sounded straight out of *Lord of the Rings*.

An Actor The Iraqi Vice-President comments:

Iraqi Vice-President This statement of President Bush is stupid.

An Actor The British Foreign Minister, Jack Straw, adds:

Straw The President's speech can be best understood by the fact there are mid-term Congressional elections coming up in November.

An Actor Condoleezza Rice is enraged:

Rice This is not about American politics, and I assume that when the British government speaks about foreign policy, it's not about British politics.

An Actor Blair instructs his personal foreign policy adviser David Manning to make a conciliatory call.

Manning and Rice are on mobile phones.

Manning The Prime Minister has asked me to apologise for his Foreign Secretary. I mean, for what his Foreign Secretary said.

Rice The President understands. This is a war, David. We know better than anyone: nobody gets it right all the time.

They laugh. At once a helicopter arrives to deposit Blair, Cherie Blair, Cherie Blair's mother, baby Leo, David Manning, Jonathan Powell and Alastair Campbell at Crawford, Texas. The Englishmen are all in dark suits with black ties. Bush, Rice and their team are all in jeans and T-shirts.

Bush Tony. Hi.

Blair George. You know David Manning?

Bush Sure do.

Blair Condoleezza. Alastair Campbell?

Campbell Of course.

Rice Hello, Alastair.

Jonathan Powell Jonathan Powell. Tony's Chief of Staff.

They turn to face a barrage of cameras.

Bush Interesting style for Texas.

Blair The Queen Mother.

Bush Ah yes. I forgot. The Queen Mother. They say a beautiful woman.

Blair Well. Yes. In her way.

They smile. Bush gestures Blair into the informal surroundings of his ranch.

An Actor In Crawford, Texas, a town which is little more than a crossroads in a scorpion-infested wilderness, the President meets Tony Blair to take him to the Prairie Chapel Ranch, his family retreat – sixteen hundred acres of oak groves, cattle, creeks and freshly stocked ponds . . .

Bush and Blair, alone, walk together in the grounds.

Bush Nobody's looking. You can undo your tie. And it's an open agenda.

Blair smiles and loosens his tie.

Blair In that case: urgently, I'd like to thank you, George, for some of the forthright things you've been saying about Israeli incursions into the Palestinian territory.

Bush Go on.

Blair I think it's important. The more even-handed America can be between Israel and the Palestinians – the fairer you can be seen to be . . .

Bush I've condemned the incursions.

Blair You have.

Bush I've told them to stop. I've told them to withdraw.

Blair You have. (*Blair waits.*) They haven't actually stopped. They haven't withdrawn.

Bush No. They haven't.

Blair waits again. Bush shrugs.

Israel's an independent nation. Sharon's a tough guy.

Blair Anyway, I think you can discern what I'm saying. You and I both have some sort of vision, I think . . .

Bush That's right . . .

Blair About how things might be reshaped in the Middle East . . .

Bush That's the very thing I want to talk to you about. That very thing.

Blair Well. The only way we're going to make progress is by bringing serious pressure. On the Israelis and the Palestinians equally. That's vital.

Bush looks at him a moment.

Bush My concern is this, Tony. At this moment, just at this very moment, I'm finding the subject of Iraq seems to be moving up the agenda.

Blair That's clear.

Bush It's moving up all the time.

Blair We've begun to sense that.

Bush I'm sitting here and since 9/11 I've been getting very strong feelings that this is something we can't leave alone.

Blair I understand those feelings.

Bush Saddam has to be dealt with. My view is, we're moving into the second phase. We did Afghanistan. Now we move on. The second phase.

Blair And I agree. There is no question of leaving him alone. He's been left alone for far too long.

Bush This is a guy who gassed his own people.

Blair Quite.

There is a short silence.

Quite. You and I want the same things.

Bush I'm sure we do.

Blair The only discussion is going to be about method. Because . . . well, back at home, you probably know, you've probably heard . . . you've been taking soundings of your own . . .

Bush Matter of fact, yes.

Blair It's true, I'm going through one of those periods – you haven't had one yet – when political problems come together.

Bush Give me an example.

Blair Well, for example, I know it sounds silly, but foxhunting. Also, there's something called Railtrack . . .

Bush Is that a railroad company?

Blair Look, you really don't want to know. My point is this: I'm in rough water, there's an accumulation – foreign and domestic. A first term is easy, George. A hundred and forty-six MPs have already signed what we call an early-day motion. It's a kind of warning. And a hundred and thirty of them are in my own party. They're expressing their opposition to British support for a US-led war on Iraq. The phrase they're using is 'deep unease'.

Bush thinks a moment.

Bush Deep unease? Huh.

Blair Now you and I know we're way ahead of ourselves.

Bush Way ahead.

Blair Any war, any conceivable war, is a long way off. It isn't going to happen tomorrow . . .

Bush Not tomorrow, no.

Blair It's an option.

Bush That's what it is. It's an option.

Blair But I have to give you my judgement.

Bush Please. I welcome your judgement.

Blair In the event of your considering armed action against Iraq, the British Parliament – and I'd say still more the British people – won't go along without UN support.

> *There is a silence.*

From the British point of view this has to be approached in a certain way. On Afghanistan you had a coalition. There were tensions, definite tensions, but we agreed on the aim. So it is here.

Bush Say more.

Blair I have an Attorney-General who is advising me that any invasion of Iraq without UN support is going to be in breach of international law.

Bush Is that what he says?

Blair That's it. That's what he says. In fact, he says more than that.

Bush Do I know this guy?

Blair You don't.

Bush Tell me what he says.

Blair What he says is this: even with UN support, any invasion may still be illegal unless we can demonstrate that the threat to British national security from Iraq is what he calls 'real and imminent'.

Bush is impassive.

Real and imminent, George. If Britain is involved, we will need evidence that Iraq can and will launch a nuclear, biological or chemical attack on a Western country. We can't go to war because of what we fear. Only because of what we know.

Bush I see. (*Bush thinks a moment.*) I see. That's putting the bar quite high.

Blair Yes. It's high.

They both think.

Now plainly, if you so choose you can set out on your own. You can do it all on your own. That's your choice. But, frankly, I wouldn't advise it.

Bush I understand.

Blair And selfishly I don't want it, because I think the whole undertaking is far too important. If we do reach the point where we one day have to contemplate military action, then I would want that action to be unarguably legitimate. I want it to have authority.

Bush Sure.

Blair And in Britain – in other parts of the world – that means the UN.

There is a silence.

Now I don't know what you feel about that. To be honest . . . if I'm honest, we're getting contradictory impressions from different parts of your administration.

Bush I can believe that.

Blair That's right. It's not unknown . . .

Bush It isn't unknown . . .

Blair We both know: a little confusion can sometimes be creative in government.

Bush It can be useful, yeah.

Blair Some of your people genuinely respect the UN. Whereas, with others, let's say, there's a contempt, an almost obsessive hatred . . .

Bush It's me that'll take the decision. I'll take the decision. I'm the President.

Blair Yeah. To me, it's an opportunity. The UN is an American-built institution. America built it.

Bush doesn't reply.

Internationally – well, in Europe, in Russia, I can help. I think I can chip in with a good deal of personal persuasion – with Chirac, with Putin. My relationships are excellent. One of the advantages of being a bit longer in office . . .

Bush Sure.

Blair Knowing the people. Knowing the personalities. I have a history, remember? Sierra Leone . . .

Bush Sure.

Blair Kosovo . . .

Bush Sure.

Blair Kosovo was a tough sell. People didn't believe in it. Believe me, I'm not scared of being unpopular . . .

Bush I know that.

Blair Going out on a limb. Military intervention for humane purposes, it's something I've believed in for a long time. I find it abhorrent, the idea the West stands by and just watches as less fortunate people suffer.

Again, Bush doesn't answer.

There's a speech of mine, in fact, I made in Chicago . . .

Bush I know that speech . . .

Blair Way before 9/11 even . . .

Bush I've read the digest.

Blair It's something I've argued. A moral duty. And I believe in it. The West has the right – no, more than a right, a responsibility – to intervene against regimes which are committing offences against their own citizens. It's simple humanity. At some point we're all going to have to articulate a new code. In my view, there's such a thing as progressive war. But when it comes to Iraq, it's difficult. Because people are asking: why Iraq? Why now? To the British, a unilateral attack is going to seem like an act of unprovoked aggression against a sovereign power. But a multilateral force, sanctioned by the UN, well, that's a different thing. That's a force for something more important than nation. That's a force for justice.

Bush nods slightly, non-committal.

Bush I'm going to think about this.

Blair Good.

Bush I'm going to talk to my people. (*Bush smiles.*) You're always eloquent, Tony.

Blair is tense now.

Blair I have one other request.

Bush Of course.

Blair There's one other thing I have to ask.

Bush Ask.

Blair We're at the beginning of a process. I've told you: I'm going to try and persuade you to go through the UN.

Bush I accept that.

Blair That means new resolutions. That means honest diplomacy. So. Nothing could be more disastrous to me – to my position – than any suggestion – any possible suggestion – from any single member of your administration – that a decision to resort to military means has already been taken. I can't describe the harm that would do.

Bush Tell me.

Blair I have to go back, I have to face my Cabinet. I have to look my colleagues in the eye and tell them the truth. I can very easily lose Cabinet members over this. If my enemies can say, 'This is a war which was cooked up a long time ago by a group in Washington who are just going through the motions . . .' If they can say, 'America decided this, they decided it, it's fixed, and nothing you do, Tony, will have any effect . . .' (*Blair pauses.*) If people can say that, then my position becomes untenable.

Bush You need to be in good faith.

Blair It's important to me.

Bush nods slightly.

Bush I've been clear with you. We're just discussing the options.

Blair Good.

Bush I can say that: we're looking at the options.

Blair Good.

Bush No war plan's on the table. It's not on the table.

Blair I think that's important. I don't just mean it's important, it's true. I know it's true. It's also important you say it.

There is a silence.

Bush It's what I'm saying.

42

Blair Good.

Bush and Blair walk out to face a press conference.

Bush Good morning. Laura and I are very honoured to have our friends, Tony and Cherie Blair and their family, visit us here in Crawford. We appreciate the rain that the Prime Minister brought with him. And so do the other farmers and ranchers in the area. Mr Prime Minister, thanks for bringing it.

Blair My pleasure, George.

Laughter.

Journalist Mr President, you have yet to build an international coalition for military action against Iraq. Has the violence in the Middle East thwarted your efforts? And Prime Minister Blair, has Bush convinced you on the need for a military action against Iraq?

Bush Adam, the Prime Minister and I, of course, talked about Iraq. We both recognise the danger of a man who's willing to kill his own people harbouring and developing weapons of mass destruction. This guy, Saddam Hussein, is a leader who gasses his own people.

Second Journalist Prime Minister, we've heard the President say what his policy is directly about Saddam Hussein, which is to remove him. Can I ask you whether that is now the policy of the British government?

Blair Well, John, you know it has always been our policy that Iraq would be a better place without Saddam Hussein. But how we now proceed in this situation, that is a matter that is open.

Bush Maybe I should be a little less direct and be a little more nuanced, and say we support regime change.

Second Journalist That's a change though, isn't it, a change in policy?

Bush No, it's really not. Regime change was the policy of my predecessor, as well.

Second Journalist And your father?

Bush You know, I can't remember that far back.

Laughter.

I think regime change sounds a lot more civil, doesn't it? The world would be better off without him. Let me put it that way, though. And so will the future.

They shake hands, wave and part.

An Actor On his return to England, Blair is restless, unsure of what's been agreed.

Blair is back in his den with Manning, Jonathan Powell and Campbell.

Blair He's tricky, isn't he?

Manning Oh yes. He's tricky.

Blair You don't know exactly what's been agreed. You don't know where you are.

Manning Cheney'll get to him. You wait.

Campbell You wait.

Manning Cheney. Rummy. Wolfie. It always happens. You agree something and then they get to him.

Blair Yes.

Manning It's a question of access.

Blair Yes.

Manning smiles.

Manning Shame we don't live there, really.

Manning stares ahead, thoughtful. Blair sips his mug of tea, seemingly casual.

An Actor Worried, uncertain, Blair issues a fatal order:

Blair I've been thinking. I've had this idea. I need – I don't know – tell me if you think this is crazy, David – I think it might help if we had some sort of dossier. A kind of *dossier.*

Manning What kind of dossier?

Blair I'd have thought, I don't know, surely the intelligence services can put something together?

Manning You mean, from sources?

Blair Just the facts. Spelt out – very simply, very clearly, about the dangers of Iraq developing and using their weapons of mass destruction.

Manning You mean we publish intelligence? The services don't like that. They don't like doing that.

Blair Yes. But this is important. This is unusual. *We* know the dangers. The public doesn't. The facts have never been marshalled, they've never been put together . . .

Manning No.

Blair In one document. I'm just thinking: I'm going to need to be armed –

Manning I see that.

Blair – with something you can actually look at . . .

Campbell It's a good idea.

Blair A4, photos, facts. Something you can actually read, you can actually look at. Hold. 'Oh, I see, there it is. That's how it is.'

There is a silence.

That's what we need. If we had that.

Manning says nothing.

Could you? Would you?

ELEVEN

The graduating class of 2002 at the United States
Military Academy at West Point passes by in a splendour
of military uniforms and martial music.

An Actor In June 2002, President Bush takes the passing-
out parade at West Point.

>   *Bush inspects the parade.*

In his address, he repudiates the core idea of the United
Nations Charter which forbids the use of force not
undertaken in self-defence. He introduces a concept new
in international law: the doctrine of the pre-emptive
strike.

>   *Bush addresses the seated graduates.*

Bush For much of the last century, America's defence
relied on Cold War doctrines of deterrence and containment. But new threats require new thinking. Deterrence –
the promise of massive retaliation against nations –
means nothing against shadowy terrorist networks with
no nation or citizens to defend. Containment is not
possible when unbalanced dictators with weapons of
mass destruction can deliver those weapons on missiles
or secretly provide them to terrorist allies.

We cannot defend America by hoping for the best.
If we wait for threats to fully materialise we will have
waited too long.

We are in a conflict between good and evil, and
America will call evil by its name. By confronting evil and
lawless regimes, we do not create a problem, we reveal a
problem. And we will lead the world in opposing it.

An Actor By August, Colin Powell has become nervous
of the direction his government is taking. On a plane

back from a tour of the Far East, he makes four pages of notes, then next day asks to see the President.

A muggy night at the White House. Bush is casually dressed. Powell and Rice are more formal.

Bush Happy to see you, Colin. Always happy to take time.

Powell This is good of you, sir.

Bush You're always welcome.

An Actor They have dinner together in the President's quarters, then afterwards:

They all settle in armchairs, relaxed.

Bush You've been where?

Powell Indonesia.

Bush That's right.

Powell The Philippines. I'm looking for a post with less foreign travel.

They all smile.

Rice Colin was saying earlier he's not sure he'd have taken the job if he'd known what it was.

Bush Why's that? Why d'you say that?

Powell Oh, simple. Aren't I always the guy who brings the bad news?

Bush looks at him a moment.

Funny, I was laughing about it with Jack Straw.

Bush That's the –

Powell Yeah. Nice man.

Bush Yeah.

Powell My opposite number.

Bush Why were you laughing?

Powell Jack was asking, 'Don't you get tired? Because it's always our job to go to the leader and say, "The French don't like it," or "The Russians won't wear it" . . .' The boss never wants to see you. Why should he see you when you're always the person telling him what he doesn't want to hear?

Bush Yeah.

Powell The opinion of foreigners.

Bush Yeah.

Powell That's what you do.

Rice Sure.

Powell You tell him what foreigners are thinking. You explain the French position. After a while, you've explained the French position so often it begins to feel like you *are* French. And you can see everyone in the room thinking: 'OK. Then why didn't you tell the French to fuck off?'

They all laugh.

'Well, why didn't you?' And it's worse in this country – it's worse for me than it is for Jack, because here everyone's also thinking: 'Hey – this is the most powerful country in the world, we're the world's only superpower, and we're wasting time while this guy tells us what some hippy Euro-peacenik foreign minister wants – why do we have to listen to him?' (*Powell looks amused.*) You can't win. In this job. You always seem weak.

Bush Not you, Colin. You don't seem weak.

The two men look at each other, level.

Tell me what's bothering you.

Powell Forgive me, sir, you'll understand, but I think I know a little about the military . . .

Bush Why, sure.

Powell One thing I know: armies make plans. That's what they do. Constantly. When you're back in the barracks, you plan. Mostly for situations which will never arise. I met an Israeli general once who told me he had a plan for the Israeli army to capture the North Pole. He thought it would work, too. It was a good plan. But that's all it was. A plan.

Bush What are you saying?

Powell I'm saying nowadays we seem to be full of plans.

There's a silence.

Bush I'm a war President. We're at war.

Powell Maybe because my whole life has been in the army I'm less impressed than some people by the use of force. I see it for what it is.

Bush What is it?

Powell Failure.

Bush smiles.

Bush I'm going to take some persuading.

Powell That's why I wanted to see you. Privately.

The two men look at each other. Bush gestures at Rice.

Bush Just Condi.

Powell All right, then I'll tell you: I'm getting frustrated by all these military plans. I can't help noticing the most enthusiastic advocates of these plans seem to be men who – strangely – weren't around last time. These men weren't on duty when their country asked them to fight.

Bush That gives you credentials. Of course it does.

Powell Armchair generals. Intellectuals. Sometimes I think all the trouble in the world is caused by intellectuals who have an 'idea'. They have some idea of action with no possible regard for its consequences. (*Powell sits forward, specific.*) We need to get a balance here.

Bush What sort of balance?

Powell Between the military and the diplomatic. Because at this moment far too little attention is being paid to the latter.

Bush Go on.

Powell If we go into Iraq without a coalition and without the UN, then we're going to find ourselves in trouble. The whole region is a tinderbox. And the current level of thinking from some people in this administration seems to be, 'OK, so let's throw in a match and see what happens . . .' It's at that level. Truly. It's nihilistic.

Powell is angry. Bush shifts.

Bush We need to make an example.

Powell I know. I know that argument.

Bush We need to do that.

Powell Sure.

Bush We need to show these people that we mean business.

Powell The Roman Empire. I'm familiar with the analogy. The Romans would always go out of their way to make an announcement: 'You are now dealing with the Roman Empire.' Yeah. So if you pricked a senator in Rome, if you just pricked him through his toga with a pin, then Roman soldiers would seek out the village you came from – wherever it was – anywhere in the empire – however far-flung – and they would kill all your family and burn down your house, they'd slaughter everyone in sight and rape all your daughters, just to make the point, just to put a message across: don't prick senators. But, sir, we're not Romans. And last time I looked at the constitution, we were still a republic, not an empire.

Bush looks chastened, as if Powell has finally reached him.

These are issues. These are large issues. And I'm the one who's going to have to pick up the pieces. (*Powell shakes his head.*) You sent me out to the Middle East to see Sharon and Arafat, I was meant to be setting out a road-map . . .

Bush OK . . .

Powell The President's much-touted new initiative for peace . . . this big road-map . . .

Bush This was unfortunate . . .

Powell And while I'm in the region, while I'm actually in the area, back home the Secretary of Defense –

Bush All right . . .

Powell – is briefing against me, he's speaking openly, saying Arafat's a busted flush and I shouldn't even be meeting him.

Bush All right, I've spoken to Donald . . .

Powell He says Colin Powell is soft on Arafat. Well, as a matter of fact Colin Powell isn't soft on Arafat – I don't have any attitude to Arafat except he's the elected leader of 3.3 million Palestinians, and my President has personally asked me to negotiate with him.

Rice It was a bad episode.

Powell You could say!

Rice None of us come well out of it.

Powell We looked like some tenth-rate African dictatorship.

Bush I spoke strongly to Donald. It's not going to happen again.

Powell It should never have happened at all! Rumsfeld cut my legs off.

There is an angry silence. Bush shifts again, uncomfortable.

OK, so I've had this experience, and now I'm looking at the current planning – planning for Iraq – and all I can see is a group of people getting a hard-on about the idea of war, and no one giving a damn for the reality. Ten times more excitement about going in than there is about how the hell we get out! (*Powell is firm now, clear.*) We invade Iraq, the whole region can be destabilised. Friends of ours like Saudi Arabia, Egypt, Jordan – all going to be put in danger. The oxygen's going to be sucked out of everything the United States is trying to do – not just the war on terror – every other diplomatic, defence and intelligence arrangement we have. And the economic implications are staggering – not least on the price of oil. In fact, there's a thousand questions nobody wants to consider, let alone answer. How will we be received? By the Iraqis themselves? Wolfowitz has some nancy-boy banker in tow. He hasn't been back to his home country for forty-four years. This guy's a certified fraud – he's on the run from embezzlement charges in Jordan – and he's the one who, from his profound ignorance of his homeland, is telling us that Iraqis are going to run out into the streets and greet us as liberators. Oh yes? And we're going on *his* word, are we? And once we go, how long will we stay? Rumsfeld wants the State Department to toy with some dicked-up plan for post-war reconstruction. Has anyone put a figure on it? And most of all, has anyone stopped for a moment – have they stopped for one moment to consider the implications? If you go into Iraq, you're going to be the proud owner of twenty-five million people. Their lives. All their hopes and aspirations. All their problems. Has anyone begun to think about that?

Powell shakes his head in disbelief.

Rice I don't understand. What do you want? You want us to do nothing?

Powell No. I want my country to be less arrogant.

Rice OK.

Powell I want us to go about this in a different way.

Bush and Rice wait for Powell to calm.

Three thousand of our citizens died. They died in an unforgivable attack. But that doesn't license us to behave like idiots. If we reach the point where everyone is secretly hoping that America gets a bloody nose, then we're going to find it very hard indeed to call on friends when we need them.

The other two are silenced by the depth of Powell's feelings. Then Bush speaks.

Bush I've said before: this isn't a popularity contest, Colin. It isn't about being popular.

Powell No, it isn't. You're right.

Bush No.

Powell It's about being effective. And the present policy of being as high-handed as possible with as many countries as possible is profoundly counter-productive. It won't work.

Bush is silent.

There's an element of hypocrisy, George. We were trading with the guy! Not long ago. People keep asking, how do we know he's got weapons of mass destruction? How do we know? Because we've still got the receipts. (*Powell shakes his head.*) It'd be nice to pretend we even have a choice. It would be great to say we can invade Iraq unilaterally. Except we can't. We need access to bases, facilities. Overflight rights. For that you need allies. Not allies you buy, not allies you bribe: allies you can actually trust, because they believe in what you're doing and they're signed up to it. We need a coalition. And if that takes time, amen. And the only place to do it is at the UN. With the help of a new UN resolution.

Bush gets up. The other two follow.

Bush I'm not going to decide on this. I'm not going to decide on this tonight.

Powell I'm going to remind you, sir. Sixty-four per cent of the American public favour this. So long as it's with the support of the international community. Without that support, the figure drops to thirty-three.

Bush I've seen the figures. They showed me the polls.

Powell OK, I'm arguing it as principle. But whatever – even as politics – go to the UN and you take the American people with you. You might even avoid war. You say I'm always looking for a downside, but I can't see the down-side of that. (*Powell turns to Rice.*) You going my way?

Rice I am.

Powell I'll run you home.

Powell turns back to Bush.

Bush Sounded like you'd been waiting a long time.

Powell I'm sorry?

Bush To say what you said.

Powell Probably thirty years.

They both smile.

Goodnight, sir.

Bush Goodnight.

Bush goes. Powell and Rice walk together down deserted White House corridors.

Rice That was good stuff.

Powell Thank you.

Rice We need a few more evenings like that.

Powell looks at her sideways. He can't tell if she supports him.

Powell It's past his bedtime, isn't it?

Rice Yes. Yes. He likes to be in bed by ten.

They walk on. Silence. Then:

Listen, if you don't mind, I'm going to take a rain check. I'm going to work a little longer.

Powell Sure. You do that. (*Powell nods.*) Goodnight, then.

Rice Goodnight.

The stage darkens. The White House glows in the night, creamy, surreal. An August evening in a Southern town.

TWELVE

The image holds, floating, dream-like. An Actor speaks quietly.

An Actor So it was. In August, the decision was taken. The United States would go back to the United Nations to demand a new resolution setting out guidelines for fresh weapons inspections and promising harsh penalties if Baghdad failed to co-operate.

Quietly, the NSC begins to reassemble – Bush, Powell, Rice, Tenet, etc. Rumsfeld comes in with Cheney.

Rumsfeld You're looking cheerful, Dick.

Cheney Am I?

Rumsfeld For a man who just lost.

Cheney Did I lose?

Everyone has taken their place at the table. They close their eyes.

Bush Oh God, guide us and guide the USA, that the righteous may triumph and we may do good, in thy name, oh Lord.

All Amen.

Bush smiles.

Bush Good morning, gentlemen. I've had a special request. The Vice-President has asked if he can speak first. Kind of a special occasion. We don't often hear from Dick, do we?

Rumsfeld Not at length.

Bush Pretty special when he speaks, never mind first.

Everyone laughs.

Fire away, Dick.

Cheney Well . . . the President's made a decision. I'm going to stand by that decision, even though I've argued against it.

Bush You certainly have.

Cheney I don't think anyone in this room begins to understand what we've let ourselves in for. But. The decision's been taken and I'm going to offer a notion of how it should be presented. I mean, to the world.

Bush Go on.

Cheney The way we do this is: crisis at the UN.

Bush Say that again.

Cheney Crisis at the UN. (*Cheney smiles.*) We turn it round, see? That's my notion. Nothing to do with American intentions. No longer a question of American foreign policy – its wisdom, its legality. No. Saddam Hussein has violated seventeen UN agreements. The UN has 173 pages of concerns about weapons of mass destruction. Therefore. The only question is: 'Does the UN still have a role?' That's the question. Is the UN an East River chattering factory? Is it an expensive irrelevance? Is this or is this not an organisation which still has the authority to enforce its own resolutions? Does it have the chops? (*Cheney looks round.*) Yes, we'll go through the UN. We go to the UN. We walk right in that glass door. Yes, we're supporting the UN. 'What, us? Sure, we support the UN.' But all the time we're asking the question: 'Can the UN deliver?'

There is a silence.

Bush I think it's good. This way it's not about us. It's about them. That's good. We put the monkey on Annan's back.

Nobody moves for a moment. A wind begins to blow. Two anoraked figures with walking sticks appear, blinking genially in the wind. They are Hans and Eva Blix.

Blix I had been walking in Patagonia with my wife in January 2000. We were on our way to the Antarctic. At a sweet town called El Calafate – it means 'The Blueberry' – I was waiting for a plane to Ushuaia – it's the southern-

57

most town in the world – when I was given a message from a Mr Kofi Annan, please to call him. The telephonist had never heard of him.

Kofi Annan at the United Nations is having to raise his voice on the telephone.

Annan Hello. Hello, I'm trying to speak to Mr Hans Blix. He's walking in Patagonia.

Blix I managed to call him back. Kofi asked me if I'd be interested in resuming my old job of leading the Iraqi weapons inspections. (*Blix hesitates for only a moment.*) I said yes. I'd be interested.

End of Act One.

Act Two

THIRTEEN

*A Palestinian Academic waits for the audience to return.
She speaks when they are ready.*

Palestinian Academic For the Palestinian, there is no
other context. We see everything in the context of Palestine.

Why Iraq? The question has been asked a thousand
times. And a thousand answers have been given. Why
was the only war in history ever to be based purely on
intelligence – and doubtful intelligence at that – launched
against a man who was ten years past his peak of
belligerence?

Why Iraq? Why now? Here comes the familiar list of
explanations. Because an Arab democracy would serve
as a model. Because it was unfinished business – 'He tried
to kill my dad.' Because Osama bin Laden had served
notice on the dictatorship in Saudi Arabia, and now
America needed a new military base. Because Cheney
worked for Halliburton. 'It was all about oil!'

For us, no. For Palestinians, it's about one thing:
defending the interests of America's three-billion-dollar-
a-year colony in the Middle East.

This is a President whose knowledge of Palestine is
confined to one helicopter flight in the company of
Sharon, from which he looked down on the suffering of
the refugees. UN resolutions which are offered as the
gold standard to legitimise war on Iraq are ignored when
they conflict with the territorial advancement of Israel.
Justice and freedom are the ostensible cause of the West –
but never extended to a people expelled from their land
and forbidden any right to return. Terror is condemned,
but state-sanctioned murder is green-lit.

The Jewish poet Chaim Nahman Bialik dreamt of a state where there would be Zionist murderers, Zionist prostitutes, Zionist crooks. Israel, he said, would only be normal when it was as corrupt and human as any other state in the world. Well, it's human now.

The victims of the conflict have become the problem. We are the Jews of the Jews.

FOURTEEN

Fleets of black cars. Angry hooting and honking. NYPD out in force. Urban chaos.

An Actor September 12th 2002. Gridlock on the streets of New York. A motorcade glides towards the glass matchbox on Sutton Place. In his hand, George Bush has the bitterly contested text of what some say will be the most important speech of his life.

Bush You know, you've got to remember, every speech is now 'the speech of my life'. I've had about six of those from my trusted advisers. So I'm immune to the 'speech of your life' stuff.

An Actor In the dog days of August, members of his administration have been on a linguistic offensive which seems to Colin Powell seriously at odds with what has been agreed –

Powell We had an agreement! I thought we had an agreement!

Dick Cheney moves into a TV studio.

An Actor To Powell's dismay the airwaves are full of colleagues aiming to discredit the principle of a return to inspections:

Cheney A return of inspectors would provide no assurance whatsoever of Saddam's compliance with UN resolutions. On the contrary, there is a great danger that it would provide false comfort that Saddam was somehow 'back in the box'.

An Actor Cheney pre-empts the findings of any future inspections:

Cheney Simply stated, there is no doubt that Saddam Hussein now has weapons of mass destruction.

Rumsfeld appears before a Senate hearing.

An Actor At a Senate hearing, Donald Rumsfeld joins in. When asked by Senator Mark Dayton:

Dayton What is compelling us now to make a precipitous decision and take precipitous action?

Rumsfeld What's different? What's different is three thousand people got killed.

The Senate hearing disappears.

An Actor Paul Wolfowitz throws in his own definition of weapons of mass destruction:

Wolfowitz It's like the judge said about pornography: I can't define it but I will know it when I see it.

An Actor Cheney goes on to make a direct connection between the attack on the Twin Towers and Saddam Hussein.

Cheney Success in Iraq means we will have struck a blow right at the heart of the base, if you will, the geographic base of the terrorists who had us under assault now for many years, but most especially on 9/11.

An Actor He asserts:

Cheney Many of us are convinced that Saddam will acquire nuclear weapons fairly soon. Just how soon we cannot gauge.

An Actor Even Condoleezza Rice seems to side with Cheney.

Rice There will always be some uncertainty about how quickly he can acquire nuclear weapons. But we don't want the smoking gun to be a mushroom cloud.

Blair paces, sheaves of paper in hand.

An Actor On the other side of the Atlantic, Tony Blair has finally received a draft of his proposed dossier which seems to him seriously disappointing in its lack of conclusive evidence.

Blair Really! I mean, really! I mean, come on!

Manning, Campbell, Jonathan Powell and Bassett all pace, the same sheaves in hand.

An Actor Special adviser Philip Bassett writes to Alastair Campbell:

Bassett Needs much more weight, writing, detail. We need *better* intelligence material, *more* material, and better flagged-up, more *convincing* material.

An Actor On September 11th an anonymous e-mail goes round the intelligence community:

A Spook reads the e-mail on a note of rising urgency.

Spook Number Ten, through the Chairman of the Joint Intelligence Committee, want the document to be as strong as possible within the bounds of available intelligence. This is therefore a last call for any items of intelligence agencies think can and should be included! Responses needed by 12.00 tomorrow!

The door of 10 Downing Street is opened at night to admit Sir Richard Dearlove.

Blair Sir Richard. Welcome. Come in. Do.

An Actor That night, Sir Richard Dearlove, Head of MI6, visits the Prime Minister.

*Manning, Campbell, Jonathan Powell and Blair are
with Dearlove in the den.*

Blair Well?

Dearlove I do . . . I do have one new source you might be
interested in.

Blair That's why we asked you.

Dearlove It isn't corroborated. (*Dearlove shifts.*) This is
highly unusual. As you know, I don't usually like to
depend on a single supplier. There are procedures . . .

Blair Plainly.

Dearlove The protocol of intelligence . . .

Blair Essential.

Dearlove We don't like to offer information from just
one line of reporting.

Blair waits again.

We have a source who is saying that the Iraqi military are
able to deploy chemical or biological weapons within
twenty to forty-five minutes of an order to do so.

There is a moment's silence.

Blair This is a source of your own?

Dearlove Not exactly.

Blair We'll need to know more.

Dearlove It's come to us through an Iraqi organisation.

Manning An exiles' organisation?

Dearlove The original source is in the Iraqi army.

There is another brief silence.

Blair Richard, it's not in anyone's interests that this
information should be wrong.

Dearlove Clearly.

Blair If the weapons inspectors go back in, and – God forbid – any of these weapons are found not to exist, then my life as Prime Minister will become very difficult indeed.

Dearlove waits.

Can you – what I'm asking – can you promise this information is sound?

Dearlove No. No, I can't promise. It's a judgement.

Blair And what is your own judgement?

Dearlove hesitates to phrase with care.

Dearlove My judgement is that this is a significant piece of raw intelligence.

Blair nods, pleased.

Blair We'll talk more. You'll give David here the details.

Dearlove I will. Goodnight, Prime Minister.

Blair Goodnight.

Everyone says 'Goodnight'. Dearlove goes. Blair paces a few moments, thinking.

There it is.

Nobody speaks.

David? Well?

Manning You asked for something. He brought it. That's service, I suppose.

Blair considers the implications of this remark.

Blair It's an instinct, isn't it? It's a feeling.

Everyone waits for the decision.

What did he say? 'Twenty to forty-five'?

Manning Yes.

Blair Use forty-five.

Downing Street dissolves.

An Actor As the dossier is prepared, the forty-five-minute claim gains a life of its own, gathering momentum with each new draft. It is mentioned four times in the published dossier and emphasised by Blair in his own introduction.

Blair This document discloses that Saddam's military planning allows for some of the WMD to be ready within forty-five minutes of an order to use them.

An Actor It becomes a headline all over the world. That night in the London *Evening Standard*:

Evening Standard Forty-five minutes to attack!

An Actor In private, George Tenet, Head of the CIA, refers to the claim as:

Tenet The 'they-can-attack-in-forty-five-minutes' shit.

The General Assembly arrives, Powell taking his place among them.

An Actor Meanwhile in New York, George Bush walks through the glass doors, first to listen to Kofi Annan –

Annan The existence of an effective international security system depends on the Council's authority – and therefore on the Council having the political will to act.

An Actor – and then, finally, to address the General Assembly, in the presence of his Secretary of State –

Powell puts on his headphones.

– who uses headphones even though they speak a common language.

Bush steps up to the podium.

Bush makes an early claim:

Bush Should Iraq acquire fissile material, it would be able to build a nuclear weapon within a year.

An Actor Then goes on to insist:

Bush The history, the logic and the facts lead to one conclusion: Saddam Hussein's regime is a grave and gathering danger.

Delegates to the General Assembly, we have been more than patient. We've tried sanctions. We've tried the carrot of oil for food, and the stick of coalition military strikes. But Saddam Hussein has defied all these efforts and continues to develop weapons of mass destruction. The first time we may be completely certain he has a nuclear weapon is when, God forbids, he uses one.

An Actor As the speech goes on –

Bush My nation will work with the UN Security Council . . .

An Actor – Powell becomes restless, waiting for the President's promise to work through a new UN resolution. Powell checks delivery against Draft 24 of the speech, agreed the previous night.

Powell whispers to John Negroponte, US Ambassador to the UN.

Powell What's going on?

An Actor In his panic, Powell believes that Dick Cheney has deliberately removed the vital pledge.

Powell He didn't say it!

An Actor But Bush himself realises that the most important words have not appeared on the teleprompter. Two lines late he inserts the undertaking from memory.

Bush We will work with UN Security Council for the necessary resolutions.

An Actor The unscripted use of the plural –

Bush 'Necessary resolutions.'

An Actor – will unleash a process of diplomacy which will last six months.

FIFTEEN

At the Hotel Pierre, Powell is sitting at an elegant dining table with John Negroponte, Jack Straw, Jeremy Greenstock, Igor Ivanov and Sergey Lavrov. They sit in silence for a moment, white-jacketed waiters attendant. And then in comes Dominique de Villepin, accompanied by Jean-David Levitte. Everyone stands, and shakes hands.

De Villepin Good morning, gentlemen . . .

An Actor Enter the French.

Powell Everyone here knows Dominique de Villepin . . .

Straw Of course . . .

De Villepin Jean-David Levitte, our Ambassador at the UN . . .

An Actor The Hotel Pierre, New York, September 13th 2002 . . .

Powell John Negroponte, our Ambassador . . .

De Villepin John . . .

Powell Igor, Sergei . . .

Ivanov Dominique . . .

Lavrov Jean-David . . . .

De Villepin Jack . . .

Straw Dominique . . .

Powell I thought it would be useful to have some kind of meeting in advance –

De Villepin I think it's an excellent idea . . .

Powell – while we're all in New York, so we can just gently find our way to each others' positions . . . .

Straw Everyone knows Jeremy Greenstock?

De Villepin It's always a pleasure to be with Jeremy.

Greenstock Dominique. Jean-David.

De Villepin What a charming hotel. This is a charming place to meet.

Powell opens his arms to say 'Let's sit.'

Are we going to eat first?

Powell I thought not. I thought talk first, then enjoy lunch.

De Villepin Why not?

They all sit. Waiters retire.

Powell To be clear: the President obviously sees yesterday's address as an act of faith in the United Nations.

De Villepin Good.

Powell But it's also a test. A test of resolve. I'm reluctant to say that at this table we hold the future of the UN in our hands. Should the Security Council fail to get compliance from Saddam Hussein, it's going to be very bad news for the prestige and standing of the organisation.

De Villepin Yes.

Powell We see this process as clearly asking the question: how effective can the UN be?

De Villepin smiles.

68

De Villepin Shall I speak?

Ivanov You go ahead.

De Villepin Yes, I can see this is what you've been saying in public . . .

Powell I'm saying it at the Hotel Pierre . . .

De Villepin Of course you are.

Powell In private.

De Villepin Yes. But I notice you use the word 'compliance' . . .

Powell Yes.

De Villepin 'The purpose of any resolution being to enforce compliance . . .'

Powell That's right . . .

De Villepin 'To work towards the disarmament of Iraq . . .'

Powell Well?

De Villepin Forgive me, but there's a confusion here, isn't there? I listened attentively to your President's speech yesterday and I found this same confusion.

Powell What confusion is that?

De Villepin It's as if, yes, you've decided to go through a process, but you haven't quite decided what the purpose of this process is.

Powell looks at him a moment.

Powell I thought we had. I thought we'd decided.

De Villepin Have you? Look, believe me, I think I speak for all of us when I say we're delighted you're here.

Ivanov We couldn't be happier.

De Villepin All of us have had to endure the taunts of Americans who've taken to saying that the only people who believe in international organisations are the people who are weak enough to need them. The only countries who insist on international law are the countries who won't spend the money to get their way by physical force.

Powell I admit: I've heard that said.

De Villepin To be honest, in Europe we get a little tired of that kind of remark.

Powell I understand.

De Villepin Belief in the United Nations isn't a sign of weakness, it's a sign of strength.

Powell So it is for us.

De Villepin Good. (*De Villepin smiles.*) You see in the last two years, since Mr Bush came to power, there have been – what would you call them? Little signs – indicators –

Powell Yes, I know.

De Villepin What are they? *Straws in the wind?* Little gestures – like the repudiation of the Kyoto protocol on the environment, withdrawal from the Anti-Ballistic Missile Treaty, rejection of the comprehensive Test Ban Treaty, repudiation of the protocol to the Biological Weapons Convention, refusal to recognise or take part in the International Criminal Court – presumably so that your Mr Kissinger can continue climbing onto aeroplanes without fear of arrest . . .

Powell Very funny . . .

De Villepin Call us over-sensitive, but some of us find it hard to believe you're now getting wholeheartedly behind the idea of international law.

Powell looks at him mistrustfully.

Speaking for myself – I think the world outside America has felt a little like a rejected lover these past two years. Now it's one o'clock in the morning and you're coming to our door with a bunch of flowers and whisky on your breath. You can see why some of us are feeling just a little bit cautious.

Powell We wouldn't have come if we didn't believe in it.

De Villepin No. (*De Villepin looks at Powell a moment, almost challenging him.*) However. We can't ignore the facts. Even as we sit in this room, as we start to enjoy our lunch, your Defense Secretary is already embarking on a substantial military build-up. Am I wrong?

Powell doesn't answer.

By our reckoning, by the time we get to the pastry you'll be on your way to putting some sixty thousand military personnel into the region.

Powell Certainly.

De Villepin So?

Powell Dominique, even Kofi welcomes our presence. He has no problem with it. Why should he? He sees it as a way of exerting pressure to enforce the will of the UN.

De Villepin Pressure. Of course.

Powell It's coercive diplomacy.

De Villepin If that's what it is – coercive – then of course it's welcome.

Powell Force isn't force unless you threaten to use it.

There's a chilly silence. De Villepin shifts.

De Villepin Yes. I was talking about this last night to Igor . . .

Powell You were?

De Villepin Yes. Just briefly.

Ivanov We met briefly.

De Villepin In advance of this meeting.

Powell Ah, you mean, you met in advance of the meeting in advance of the meetings?

They all smile.

De Villepin Yes, exactly.

Powell Go on.

De Villepin We were saying: you're on what I think you call a twin-track, aren't you? The military and the diplomatic.

Powell Yes. Yes, we are.

De Villepin Clearly it's going to need an extraordinary balance of skill to keep those two tracks running. Rather than crashing into each other.

Powell That's what I'm here for.

De Villepin And believe me – I wanted to say this – we're most of all pleased it's you. That means a great deal to us.

Powell Thank you. (*Powell is watchful, mistrusting De Villepin's flattery.*)

De Villepin The most popular man in America.

Powell I'm sorry?

De Villepin According to the polls.

Powell is icy.

More popular even than the President.

Powell They're just polls.

De Villepin All the same. All the same. It's not a bad thing to be, is it? More popular than your own President?

Virtually the only uncontested hero in America. It puts you in a remarkably strong position.

There is a silence. De Villepin drums his fingers on the table.

Straw Dominique, I'm an averagely intelligent person and I'm not sure where you're heading.

De Villepin No? It must be my English.

Straw Must be.

De Villepin I'll make myself clear. (*De Villepin turns to Powell, now focused.*) There's all the difference in the world between coming to the UN with the aim of getting Saddam to disarm through peaceful means, and coming to the UN in order simply to get a stamp of approval for an invasion.

Powell That's not what we're asking for.

De Villepin Isn't it?

Powell No. No, I don't think it is. I mean, we haven't yet specified the wording of the resolution . . .

De Villepin Exactly . . .

Powell That lies ahead.

De Villepin Exactly.

Powell The framing of the resolution, that's the very subject of this lunch . . .

De Villepin smiles again.

De Villepin All it is: I'm looking at this contradiction and trying to make some sense of it. On the one hand, the US says it's giving the Security Council the chance to handle the process. On the other hand, certain members of the administration – not you, Colin – are implying that only one outcome is going to be acceptable. My point is this: you can't come to the UN, then announce that the UN has failed if it gives you any result but the one you want. You can't do that. Put it another way: you can't play football and be the referee as well. That isn't – I'm using the English expression – 'playing fair'.

Powell That's not what we're doing. We're not doing that. This is a negotiation. Genuine. With equal partners. There are fifteen countries on the Security Council. We want fifteen votes. Freely given. We're in good faith.

De Villepin I would hope.

Powell Do you think I'd be here if we weren't?

De Villepin opens his hands, as if to say he doesn't know the answer.

De Villepin I'm going to make a suggestion in the hope of defusing any possible tension.

Powell Go ahead.

De Villepin Though I'm becoming embarrassed at being the only person who speaks.

Straw Believe me, we're enjoying listening.

Powell What's your suggestion?

De Villepin smiles.

De Villepin I suggest two resolutions.

Powell Two?

De Villepin Yes. One to effect disarmament. And the second . . . the second to trigger war if, after a reasonable time, disarmament is not proved to have taken place. It seems the easiest way of disentangling your two different aims.

Powell I see. (*Powell looks at him a moment.*) I see. You want me to get a resolution, then come back and get another?

De Villepin That's it exactly.

Powell Do you . . . do you have any idea how hard it was to get here in the first place?

De Villepin I have some idea, yes.

Powell And now you want me to come back?

But De Villepin is not fazed.

De Villepin France won't consider a first resolution which contains any kind of hidden trigger, any mechanism which might trigger war. The French are genuinely delighted to help the United States if your purpose is, indeed, disarmament. Nothing would make us happier. If you have a second purpose – to license an attack – to seek international cover for an American invasion – then no. We deal with a new situation only when and as disarmament is shown not to occur.

Powell is looking at him in dismay.

Please. What I'm suggesting is not unreasonable. It can hardly come as a surprise. If you remember, your own President referred to 'resolutions' in the plural.

Negroponte That was a glitch!

De Villepin He used the plural.

Negroponte It was a technical glitch!

De Villepin Whatever.

Negroponte You know perfectly well: when the President said he was going to 'bring forward resolutions' what he meant was 'resolution'. Single.

Levitte It's a pity that's not what he said.

Negroponte He was improvising. He had to improvise. The machine went down and he did very well to say anything at all!

Levitte is taking out a transcript.

Levitte If there's a problem, I have a transcript here. I can check.

Powell There's no need to check! (*Powell has spoken with unexpected sharpness. Now he turns to De Villepin, measured, cool.*) Good. Very well. We've laid out preliminary positions, and now we're all going to eat our lunch. Afterwards I'm going to think things over.

De Villepin Thank you.

Powell Because there's some kind of contract here, I think.

De Villepin Contract?

Powell Yes. Between us. (*Powell stops, deliberate.*) Think. Consider. The questions you might have asked me: 'Do I personally want to see the inspectors back in?' 'Yes.' 'Do I genuinely want the inspections to succeed?' 'Yes'. 'Do I want war?' 'Emphatically, no.' Now if these are the outcomes we all desire, it's up to you to make my life liveable. You have to give me something I can take back to the President.

De Villepin I accept that.

Powell Push me too hard and you'll end up with an outcome the opposite of what you want. Remember that. This is a two-way street. Your good faith is to be tested as much as mine. (*Powell smiles, still chilly.*) If anyone's stupid enough to think this is payback time for whatever grudge they happen to be nursing against the US – be it Kyoto or the Criminal Court or – I don't know – how they hate McDonald's – then what they'll be doing in effect is condemning Iraqi women and children to the sort of bombardment which is going to make them wish they'd never been born. And possibly civil chaos after. That's what I'm trying to avoid. (*Powell waits for this to sink in.*) As to two resolutions, well, it's a technical question, because although we're going to fight about words, it won't ultimately be about words. It'll be a fight about attitude: wanting to help or not.

The table is silenced.

Yes, America's a great power. The only great power. You may see this as the moment when America has to submit to the international will. And you may be relishing that prospect.

De Villepin I didn't say that.

Powell But I don't see it that way. (*Powell smiles.*) I know you're a lover of history . . .

De Villepin I am . . .

Powell I think it's Hobbes, isn't it? who says 'Covenants without swords are but words . . .'

De Villepin I think it's Hobbes.

Powell So. For the moment, America has the swords and is therefore – whether we like it or not – the enforcer of covenants. In France, I don't know, you may wish for the day when that's no longer so. But, with the best will in the world, I don't see that day arriving in the next few months. (*Powell reaches across and touches De Villepin's wrist.*) We have to work together.

De Villepin We'll work together.

Powell Good. I'm going to hold you to that. (*Powell gets up to get the waiters back. He goes to the door, then turns.*) Oh, and by the way – about working together. If we do go for two resolutions – *if* – one for proof of disarmament, the other for war – I warn you now, don't vote for the first unless you're going to be ready one day to vote for the second. We'd take that very badly. (*Powell looks a moment.*) Lunch.

Powell opens the door and the waiters in white coats pour in, bearing food and drink.

SIXTEEN

Groups of Senators and Congressmen arrive to be briefed by Bush.

An Actor Soon after his address to the UN the President goes to Congress to seek the authorisation he needs. First, he embarks on a lobbying campaign, inviting a hundred and ninety-five Congressmen and all hundred Senators to the White House for personal briefings:

Bush You can't distinguish between Al Qaeda and Saddam when you talk about the war on terror.

An Actor After two days of debate in the House, the President has a vote of 266 to 133 to allow him carte blanche to deploy the US armed forces 'as he deems to be necessary and appropriate'.

The Senate assembles.

In the Senate, John McCain captures the mood:

McCain There is no greater responsibility we face than voting to place this country on a course that could send young Americans to war in her defence. All of us must weigh our consciences carefully. The very fact that we are holding this free debate serves as a reminder that we are a great nation, united in freedom's defence, and called once again to make the world safe for freedom's blessings to flourish. The quality of our greatness will determine the character of our response.

Parliament assembles.

An Actor In Britain, Parliament is recalled to debate the growing crisis. Fifty-three Labour MPs rebel. One says:

Simpson Bush will hit Iraq in much the same way that a drunk will hit a bottle – to satisfy his thirst for power and oil. I must tell the Prime Minister that the role of a friend in such circumstances is not to pass the drunk the bottle!

Blix and Mohammed ElBaradei arrive, smiling at a piece of paper they both hold.

An Actor America draws up the first draft of a startlingly tough resolution which insists on the right to send US troops into Iraq to guard inspectors as they go about their work.

Blix It was so remote from reality. It was written by someone who doesn't understand how inspections function.

Powell lifts a phone to Blix.

Powell Hans. It's Colin Powell. The President and I were thinking it would it would be nice if you dropped by to see him.

Blix I'd be delighted.

Powell We'll send a van to your hotel at 8 a.m. That way we can get you right in and avoid security.

Blix and ElBaradei walk with Powell down White House corridors. Cheney gets up and shakes their hands. They all sit down.

An Actor Hans Blix and his colleague Mohammed ElBaradei are invited to the White House. First, they are taken to the Vice-President's office for what turns out to be a brief meeting

Cheney You know, we're sure there are weapons there. I don't think you're going to have any trouble finding them. And if you do have any trouble, understand, we're ready to discredit you.

Everyone gets up.

An Actor Moments later, they are ushered into the Oval Office.

Bush gets up from behind the desk to shake hands.
Powell hovers.

Bush It's a great honour to meet you both. I'm honoured to meet you, sir.

Blix No, the honour is mine.

ElBaradei Good morning, Mr President.

Bush gestures them to sit down.

Bush I'm hearing you're thinking you can start in two months.

Blix Two months, yes. We've known for some time we might go back in. So it's a practical question. Reassembling the team.

Bush sits back behind his desk.

Bush A lot of things get said, there's a lot of noise in the air, hyperventilation, this is – you know – stuff that goes on. I tune it out. I don't listen. They say I'm a mad Texan bent on war. That's not so. That's what I wanted to say to you. I want to go through the UN and I want him disarmed.

Blix I'm happy to hear that.

Bush We have confidence in you.

Blix Thank you, Mr President. That means a great deal to us.

Bush nods and looks at him a moment.

Bush You can be assured, Mr Blix, you've got the force of the United States behind you.

Blix Yes.

Bush The only mistake you could make is to imagine that when you come to report, it's you that's making the decision. About whether to take further action.

Blix Of course not. I agree with you. That's not my role.

Bush No. It isn't you that makes that decision. It's me.

They all get up.

An Actor Blix and ElBaradei are now ushered into a third and final meeting, this time with Condoleezza Rice.

They all sit down.

Rice What I want to put to you, is: it's understood, you work for the UN, they're your masters, we accept that. But we feel there can also be input from individual members of the Security Council.

Blix Which members do you have in mind?

Rice Naturally, the United States.

Blix nods, as if thinking seriously.

Blix What sort of input? I mean, intelligence, yes, the more the better. Materiel. We're grateful. But beyond that?

Rice This is a very big job, it's an important job . . .

Blix Believe me, I don't need persuading . . .

Rice And we have a lot of ideas on how you can be helped.

Blix Helped?

Rice Yes. We're proposing some sort of philosophical agreement. On paper. A signed agreement. About what you're going to do. And the way you're going to do it.

Blix nods again, considering.

Blix I don't think I can do that, Dr Rice. I work for the UN.

Blix stares at her. Wolfowitz comes in.

An Actor Later, in the meeting, Paul Wolfowitz arrives.

Rice You don't know Paul Wolfowitz?

Blix I haven't had the pleasure. How do you do?

Elbaredei, Blix and Wolfowitz stand round shaking hands.

An Actor Nine months earlier Wolfowitz has ordered a secret CIA investigation to discredit Hans Blix.

Wolfowitz has sat down and is looking hard at Blix.

Wolfowitz You do know they have the weapons, don't you? I mean, you are starting from that position, I hope?

Blix I go in with a great deal of knowledge.

Wolfowitz It's not your knowledge, it's your position I'm interested in.

Blix My position?

Wolfowitz Yes. What's your position? What is it?

Blix Well, I have experience, I hope I have judgement, but professionally, I see it as a matter of principle: I have no position.

Wolfowitz just stares at him.

Wolfowitz You remember, the problems we had last time . . .

Blix I do.

Wolfowitz Last time we couldn't get scientists to travel abroad.

Blix It's true. It's always a problem.

Wolfowitz Everyone's terrified. If you leave the country to talk to you guys, then Saddam will kill you when you get back. He'll kill your family. It's a dictatorship.

Blix I agree.

Wolfowitz So I've been thinking about it. I've got a solution.

Blix We'd like to hear it.

Wolfowitz It'll work like a subpoena. A sort of international subpoena. We have the right to slap an injunction on a scientist, we take him out, we talk to him abroad and this time we get what we need.

Blix says nothing.

What do you think?

Blix Forgive me, but somehow I've never seen the UN as being in the kidnapping business.

They all shake hands, making polite goodbyes.

Rice It's been a great privilege to meet you.

Blix It's certainly been a very useful meeting.

An Actor Colin Powell spends the next four weeks in negotiation after the first US draft is rejected by all fourteen other members of the Security Council. After seven weeks, arguments about wording have reached a bitter stand-off. The French insist that there may be serious consequences should Iraq be in material breach of the resolution, as evidenced by:

Levitte A false declaration 'and' a general failure to cooperate.

An Actor The Americans prefer the word:

Negroponte 'Or'.

An Actor The dispute over this single word lasts five days.

Rice is in her office at night. Powell appears.

Powell Condi . . . You busy?

Rice I'm busy. Busy enough. Come in.

They both smile.

How you getting on? You close?

Powell Still that word.

Rice The President's very firm about this. Lose the little things, you start losing the big ones.

Powell nods slightly.

Powell Condi, the French aren't stupid. They know we'll go to war if we have to.

Rice So?

Powell I'm trying to avoid war.

Rice We're all trying to avoid war.

Powell Yeah. (*Powell looks at her, not believing her.*) Look, they're offering a formula. It's words. Words set out in a certain order. It satisfies their honour and it satisfies us. They're going to say we need a second resolution, we're going to say we don't. You can read it either way.

Rice That good, eh?

They both smile.

Powell All we want is a headline: 'US Achieves Iraq Resolution'. I can get fourteen votes . . .

Rice Fourteen?

Powell Maybe fifteen. Even Syria. Who knows? But I have to give in to the French. On this one thing. It's a way of saying, 'Look, we're not going to give you nothing.'

Rice stares, undecided.

We were going to do this in two weeks, remember? Do we want it to take longer? Do we want it to fail? I don't think so.

Rice Do you like this guy?

Powell He's a self-defined intellectual who writes biographies of Napoleon. He destroyed my daughter's wedding to discuss 'and' or 'or'.

Rice You like him.

Powell looks her in the eye.

Powell Condi, I'm telling you: he gave me his word.

Rice OK.

Powell That means something.

They stare at one another a moment.

Do you think . . . do you think you could speak to the President?

Rice Why don't you speak to him?

They both know the answer, so neither speaks.

Powell No point in being a trusted adviser unless she gives some trusted advice.

Rice smiles in assent.

Thank you.

Powell goes. Rice sits alone.

An Actor On November 8th Powell concedes the word 'or' and the Security Council unanimously adopts Resolution 1441. Immediately afterwards the Americans and the French brief the press, giving contradictory readings of the same document.

Diplomats at the UN brief separate pools of journalists.

Negroponte Resolution 1441 contains no hidden triggers and does not constrain any member state from taking any action to defend itself against the threat posed by Iraq.

Levitte By insisting on two stages, the resolution makes it clear that it is only the Security Council which can handle this matter.

An Actor Dominique de Villepin adds:

De Villepin I have signed nothing which locks us in to war.

An Actor This is widely seen as the moment of Powell's greatest triumph.

SEVENTEEN

General Hassan Muhammad Amin sets out a table with twelve thousand pages of documents for the world's press to photograph.

An Actor Within the required week, Iraq re-admits inspectors and commits to producing a full description of their chemical facilities within thirty days. On December 7th, General Hassan Muhammad Amin has a photo call.

A media scrum, flash photos and a proud General.

Piled on a table are forty-three spiral-bound volumes of documents, containing 12,159 pages, six folders and twelve CD-ROMs.

Amin We are a country devoid of weapons of mass destruction.

An Actor Saddam Hussein makes a statement on Iraqi television:

Saddam speaks in Arabic, a translator renders it in English.

Saddam We apologise to God about any act which has angered him in the past, and that was held against us, and we apologise to the Kuwaitis on the same basis.

An Actor Amin then drives to the UN compound and hands the papers over. They are thence flown on to the UN in New York.

Another media scrum as two young men arrive with huge bags.

The US insists that the submission will be a cookbook for lethal chemical weapons and rules that not all members of the Council can be trusted to read the whole document.

Blix To be honest, I was happy for the document to go first to Washington. They have the logistical capacity to make fifteen copies of twelve thousand pages. We don't.

An Actor During the week in Washington the names of the two companies which, before the 1991 Gulf War, secretly supplied Iraq with seventeen types of biological agents are removed. One company is American. The other French.

In Blair's den, Jonathan Powell and Manning sit reading a résumé. Blair pacing moodily, the same résumé in hand. Campbell sitting at a desk, quietly working.

Blair I don't know. I just don't know. I knew it'd be bad, but not this bad!

Manning It's bad.

Blair He's blown it. He's really blown it, hasn't he? I thought Saddam would give us *something*. I did genuinely believe he'd give us *something*.

Manning Twelve thousand pages – the whole thing a pointless re-hash.

Blair The Americans are going to go crazy. They're going to say he's not in compliance . . .

Manning Cheney, Rummy, Wolfie . . .

Blair Exactly. He's playing into their hands. They're all going to say, 'Oh great, now we can go to war!' I mean, really! This was Saddam's chance. Why didn't he take it?

Campbell Because he's got the IQ of parsley.

But Blair ignores this, pacing.

Blair And now where are we? Blix is running round Mesopotamia like Hercule Poirot. The whole world is watching and everyone seems to think it's some kind of game. Everyone thinks: 'If Blix doesn't find the weapons, then Saddam wins.' The man is a murderous dictator, and we've turned the whole thing into Cluedo. Tell me I'm wrong.

Manning You're not wrong.

Blair shakes his head.

Blair It's all Blix's fault. He's letting himself be used. Why can't people understand? It isn't Blix's job to find the weapons – it's Saddam's job to prove they've been destroyed.

Manning Of course.

Blair It's perfectly simple. Why don't people get it? I've explained it. God knows I've explained it.

Campbell You have. Often.

Blair It's not up to us to prove they exist! It's up to them to prove they don't!

Manning looks at his fingernails, the diplomat.

Manning There was always a danger. We knew that. We went in knowing that inspections could be misconstrued.

Blair David, I promised the British people: no war without the UN. (*Blair moves away, insistent.*) There's one rule. With the Americans there's one rule. You get in early. The earlier you join, the more influence you have. You prove your loyalty. And that way they listen.

Manning It's true.

Blair You remember what happened to Kinnock?

Manning I do.

Blair My God! The humiliation! Ronald Reagan gave him twenty minutes! We're a Labour government. The one thing we've learnt: if for a moment, if even for a moment we come adrift from Washington, our credibility is gone. It's gone!

Campbell looks up as Blair paces.

I've got my military saying to me, 'Are we in or are we out?' They're saying, 'We need time to prepare.' And I've got the British public saying, 'You promised you'd wait.' I've got the British public saying, 'Well you haven't found the weapons, so you can't be going to war.' How many times can I lift the phone? How many times can I say, 'George, hold on, just hold on . . .' (*Blair bursts out again at the injustice.*) Saddam was meant to give me something! He was meant to help!

Manning Yes. Yes. It's tricky.

Blair I can't believe where we are. Every bad thing that could have happened has happened.

The advisers are looking one to another, lost for advice. Powell is quiet, conciliatory.

Jonathan Powell You think the world's reasonable, Prime Minister. It's not reasonable.

Blair I'm not asking Saddam to be clever. I'm just asking him to have some elementary cunning. Some vestigial instinct for survival. At least have that! Every politician has that! (*Blair looks away, lost.*) What am I meant to do?

Manning You have to do what you're doing. You have to leave it with Blix.

Blair shakes his head.

Blair It's wrong. It's so wrong.

Downing Street disappears.

An Actor In the second week of the New Year, Rice flags up an issue which has been disturbing her.

The Oval Office, Bush alone at his desk. Rice comes in.

Rice There's something I need to mention to you, sir.

Bush Whatever.

Rice An imbalance.

Bush Tell me.

Rice It's my job to balance out separate needs, separate requirements. The different departments. To listen. As of this moment, the Secretary of Defense knows your plans, sir. Donald's been party to them. You could say, some time back. (*Rice waits a moment.*) The Secretary of State doesn't know your plans.

Bush I understand.

Rice He's not been party to them. (*Rice shifts.*) Colin works every day . . .

Bush Yes.

Rice At the UN.

Bush Yes.

Rice Among foreign ministers. Hitting the phones. Taking the diplomatic route.

Bush Yes.

Rice I'm not sure this situation can go on as it is.

Bush stares, at his most enigmatic. Rice goes.

An Actor On January 13th, Powell is summoned to the Oval Office.

Bush gets up as Powell arrives.

Bush Welcome, Colin.

Powell Mr President.

Bush Come in. Make yourself comfortable.

Powell Alone?

Bush Yes.

Powell No Condi?

Bush No. No Condi.

Powell has said it lightly, but Bush's tone alerts him. Tense, he sits.

Powell Sir?

Bush Colin, I think we've reached a fork in the road. We're at that fork. I don't think there's a way round this. These inspections are a distraction. They weaken us. They weaken our purpose.

Powell looks at him a moment.

Powell In what way?

Bush We've got ourselves into a situation where we're insisting he's guilty until he proves he's innocent. That's not good. That's not good for us. He's making a monkey of us.

Powell What you're saying: you've made up your mind.

Bush I'm saying that.

Powell You've thought this through?

Bush nods.

Bush I've taken a decision. If you have a problem with that decision, best thing is you should speak. You should say something now. I've invited you in. I'm giving you the chance to say something now.

They look at each other. There is a long silence.

It would be a big thing. It would be a big thing if you disagreed. Well?

Powell I don't disagree.

Bush nods, satisfied. Powell gets up.

Thank you, sir. Thank you for telling me. (*Powell goes out.*)

An Actor Later, Bush recalls:

Bush It was a very cordial conversation. I would describe it as cordial. I think the log will show that it was relatively short.

An Actor White House records show that the encounter lasted twelve minutes.

Bush, alone, looks at us a moment.

Bush I didn't need his permission.

EIGHTEEN

A Brit in New York appears.

Brit in New York 'America changed.' That's what we're told. 'On September 11th everything changed.' 'If you're not American, you can't understand.'

The infantile psycho-babble of popular culture is grafted opportunistically onto America's politics. The language of childish entitlement becomes the lethal rhetoric of global wealth and privilege.

Asked how you are as President, on the first day of a war which will kill around thirty thousand people: 'I feel good.'

I was in Saks Fifth Avenue the morning they bombed Baghdad. 'Isn't it wonderful?' says the saleswoman. 'At last we're hitting back.' 'Yes,' I reply. 'At the wrong people. Somebody steals your handbag, so you kill their second cousin, on the grounds they live close. Explain to me,' I say, 'Saudi Arabia is financing Al Qaeda. Iran, Lebanon and Syria are known to shelter terrorists. North Korea is developing a nuclear weapons programme. All these you leave alone. No, you go to war with the one place in the region admitted to have no connection with terrorism.' 'You're not American,' says the saleswoman. 'You don't understand.'

Oh, a question, then. If 'You're not American. You don't understand' is the new dispensation, then why not 'You're not Chechen'? Are the Chechens also now licensed? Are Basques? Theatres, restaurants, public squares? Do Israeli milk-bars filled with women and children become fair game on the grounds that 'You don't understand. We're Palestinian, we're Chechen, we're Irish, we're Basque'? If the principle of international conduct is now to be that you may go against anyone you like on the grounds that you've been hurt by somebody else, does that apply to everyone? Or just to America?

On September 11th, America changed. Yes. It got much stupider.

NINETEEN

Rice welcomes Maurice Gourdault-Montagne and Jean-David Levitte to her office.

An Actor On the very same day that Powell is informed of his President's intentions, Condoleezza Rice entertains Chirac's personal envoy, Maurice Gourdault-Montagne, nicknamed MGM, accompanied by Ambassador Levitte.

MGM President Chirac sends his compliments.

93

Rice Please send him mine. D'you mind if we eat in the office?

They move to a small lunch table.

An Actor At lunch, the French run through their reservations. At the end of the meal:

MGM Forgive me, but my sense is that even if a decision to invade hasn't actually been taken, it is at least imminent. Please, I don't expect you to comment. (*Gourdault-Montagne puts up a hand.*) France came here to express our anxieties. We've expressed them. But thanks to the skill of Mr Powell, France has so far managed to avoid having to take up a position of public opposition to American plans.

Rice We've noted that. We're grateful.

MGM My President feels that it's in neither country's interest that France and America quarrel.

Rice We don't want that either.

MGM Nobody wants it. These are two great countries. Two of the greatest countries in the world.

Rice Are you making a deal?

Levitte We're making an offer.

Rice I see. Carry on.

MGM You have one reading of Resolution 1441. We have another. We've made our point. Put it like this: we have no desire, we have no need to go on making it.

Rice frowns.

Rice All right. Let's be clear. You're saying . . .

MGM We're saying we would happy to help the temperature to fall.

Rice We'd certainly appreciate that.

94

MGM We're happy to be silent.

Rice That would be welcome.

MGM We agree. Why force an issue which doesn't need to be forced?

They wait a moment while Rice takes this in.

Levitte Naturally, the only problem . . .

MGM Yes . . .

Levitte The only problem would be if anyone were stupid enough to try and bring forward a second resolution.

MGM Yes.

Levitte We would take that badly.

MGM Yes.

Levitte The first was difficult enough.

The Frenchmen smile.

Rice I don't understand. It was you who insisted on a second resolution in the first place. It was France.

MGM That's right.

Rice Now you seem to be saying you're happy to let it go.

Levitte That's right. Why not? The French are realists. We see how the future is likely to develop. A second resolution and France would be put in an impossible position. France would be forced to use its veto, which it has no wish to do.

Rice No.

MGM What our President is saying is: if you wish to declare the diplomatic process over, France will have no problem with that.

Rice Thank you.

There is a silence.

Thank you.

The Frenchmen leave. Rice goes to Powell's office.

An Actor At once Rice goes to see Powell.

Powell No. It's not going to work. We can't do it. Blair!

Rice It's always Blair.

Powell Blair promised a second resolution. He doesn't have a choice. Nor does Howard in Australia. Nor does Aznar. They're fighting their own public.

Rice is about to speak. Powell cuts her off.

Blair's swimming upstream, Condi. We can't let him drown.

They look at each other a moment.

An Actor The news of the rejection of their offer is conveyed to the French. One week later:

De Villepin on the phone to Powell.

De Villepin Colin, we were wondering if you were going to come to New York. We're calling a special meeting –

Powell I know . . .

De Villepin – of foreign ministers in the Security Council. To discuss global terrorism. I think it's going to look odd if you're not there.

Powell Dominique, the meeting's on January 20th.

De Villepin Yes, I'm sorry about that.

Powell It's not . . . I have a number of speaking engagements. It's also . . .

De Villepin Yes?

Powell is reluctant to speak.

Powell It's Martin Luther King day.

Silence. Neither man moves.

An Actor On January 20th Powell travels specially to New York. The session passes unremarkably but afterwards, in front of the world's press and without prior warning, France publicly hardens its position.

Press mob. De Villepin holds up his hands.

De Villepin Gentlemen, gentlemen . . .

An Actor The incident is known in diplomatic circles as 'the ambush'.

De Villepin raises his voice.

De Villepin We believe today that nothing justifies military intervention. Military action is a dead end. Nothing justifies an American adventure. Nothing! Nothing!

Journalist Will France use its veto in the case of any new resolution?

De Villepin France is a permanent member of the Security Council. It will shoulder all of its responsibilities faithful to all the principles it has.

An Actor In response, the American people go into a frenzy of French-bashing. French tourism, French wine, French fries.

Powell is raging round his office.

Powell What is this? What the hell is this? I've got a bunch of right-wing nutcases in the White House, I've got the treacherous French in the Security Council. I'm standing in the fucking road! And the shit is all flowing one way! (*Powell turns incensed.*) We had an agreement! I thought we had an agreement!

Donald Rumsfeld is surrounded by the press mob.

An Actor Happy to see the row escalate, Donald Rumsfeld fans the flames when asked about European dissent:

Rumsfeld You're thinking of Europe as Germany and France. I don't. That's old Europe. If you look to the east, Germany has been a problem, France has been a problem. But you look at the vast numbers of other countries in Europe. They're not with France and Germany on this, they're with the United States.

An Actor As a deliberate provocation, a few days later he proclaims:

Rumsfeld There are four countries that will never support us. Never. Cuba, Libya and Germany.

An Actor Asked to name the fourth:

Rumsfeld I forgot the fourth.

The press mob go.

An Actor Noticing a sudden hardening in Colin Powell's attitudes, a reporter asks:

Reporter You've now become a hawk in Iraqi issues and speak just like Rumsfeld, so why did you change?

An Actor Powell replies:

Powell It's very unwise to stereotype people with one-word labels.

TWENTY

The Oval Office. Bush is already there, as Rice, Powell, Rumsfeld and Cheney assemble quickly and sit down.

Rice Gentlemen, good morning. The President's called this meeting – informal meeting – because we have a problem to discuss. Prime Minister Blair's going to be here in twenty-four hours. And he's going to be making a request.

Cheney smirks.

Cheney Yeah, I think we know what that request is going to be.

Rice And we have to take it seriously because – clearly – he's our principal ally. He's committed. He's committed to the cause.

Bush turns to Powell.

Bush Colin?

Powell Well, I think as everyone's guessed . . .

Rumsfeld Yeah, we've guessed . . .

Powell Blair is going to be asking us to help him secure a second resolution. Which he needs for domestic political reasons.

Bush How you feeling about that, Colin?

Powell I'll tell you frankly, sir, I don't relish the prospect. But on the other hand . . . I want to see diplomacy exhausted. I don't want to see it terminated.

Bush turns to Cheney.

Bush Dick?

Cheney I don't know. I don't understand what we're doing. We've got a resolution, haven't we?

Powell Yeah. 1441.

Cheney If you remember, I didn't want to go get that one . . .

Rice We remember . . .

Cheney But at least we got it, and now – I'm trying to make sense of this – don't we look stupid if we go back for another?

Powell Well . . .

Cheney In fact, go back for a second, the only thing we're doing is admitting that the first one didn't give us authorisation in the first place.

Powell That's not so. We're not admitting that. I'm making that plain.

Cheney ignores him, gathering force.

Cheney In fact, can I ask something here? Exactly what craziness are we getting ourselves into? I see no logic. If the first one was good enough – which we always said it was – what the fuck is the point of a second?

Powell It's not us that needs it.

Cheney Exactly. So OK, so we go back, do we? We put ourselves back in the diplomatic mudpit, is that right? And we say, 'The first is fine, the first is just beautiful, but now we've decided we'd like a second, just like the cream and nuts on top of the sundae – so the dish *looks* better.' I mean, are we serious?

Rumsfeld We're not serious.

Cheney We're going to war! The whole country's furious with the French. They're furious with the Germans. We've got the resolution. We've got the troops. Let's go!

Cheney has sounded final and now his emotion is infectious.

Rumsfeld Can I say something? With respect, sir. Isn't this moment now for a little reality? Before we commit? Before we commit young Americans to give their lives? Isn't this the moment just to do the obvious thing and maybe stop listening to Europe? Because we can see – we're getting used to this – Europeans are always more worried about how exactly America *reacts* to the threat of Saddam than they are about Saddam himself. Man's coming at you with a knife. All they're worrying about is which hand we use to take it away.

Powell But *is* he coming at us? We believe he is. But we've got to persuade everyone else. By facts. It's not such a terrible instinct, Donald. People want things to be legitimate.

Rumsfeld I'll tell you what's legitimate. What we do is legitimate. Read the American Constitution. It was written by Thomas Jefferson and he said – and I'll remind you of his words – that what makes governments legitimate is the consent of the people.

Cheney That's right.

Rumsfeld The authority to act comes from the will of the people.

Cheney The American people.

Rumsfeld That's right. (*Rumsfeld speaks from deep, suppressed emotion.*) Power in this country doesn't come from its institutions, and it sure as hell doesn't come from abroad. There's a lot of talk going on about 'The UN wants this' and 'The UN's allowing that'. Well no, actually. And once we start thinking like that, we're dead.

Powell I'm not thinking like that.

Rumsfeld The United Nations has no power, nor is it meant to.

Powell Of course not.

Rumsfeld It's a facility. That's all it is. It's a setting, it's a context. The United Nations never achieved anything, not in or of itself. Something isn't right because the UN says it is. (*Rumsfeld is quiet, persuasive.*) I know why we're going to war. And so do you, Colin. Because the man is a lunatic and we can't afford the risk that one day he might team up with terrorists.

Bush That's what it is.

Rumsfeld Yeah.

Bush It's about risk.

Rumsfeld That's what it's about. In this new world, in this new post-9/11 world. (*Rumsfeld shakes his head.*) And that is something which all grown-up people understand.

Cheney Everyone understands.

Rumsfeld Yeah. Which is why the dishonesty gets to me.

Cheney Sure.

Rumsfeld It gets to me.

Cheney It gets to me as well.

Rumsfeld Because what can you say about these people in Europe except that they live their lives under the American umbrella? Every time it rains they come running for shelter. And yet they still think that they're entitled to say, 'Hey you're not holding that umbrella right.' Or more often, 'I want a share of that umbrella.' Or even, 'You're not allowed an umbrella because not everybody's got one.' And that's the dishonesty, that's the rank dishonesty.

Cheney It's such dishonesty.

Rumsfeld They talk about the American empire! How can we be an empire? Who ever heard of an empire that spends day after day discussing exit strategies? (*Rumsfeld shakes his head.*) We don't need lectures from Europe on how to hold our knives and forks. (*Rumsfeld turns back to Powell.*) They pretend all the time that they're upset because we're not consulting. 'They're not consulting,' they say! Are you fooled by that? I'm not. Because what they really hate, what's really bugging them, is not the *way* we do things. It's that we're the only people in the world that can do them. It's not our manner, it's our power. And all they want, all anyone wants, is to put a brake on that power. And that is the purpose of this exercise. That is the purpose of getting us snared up in yet another fucking resolution.

Powell is not buying it.

Powell This is different.

Rumsfeld Why? Why's it different?

Powell Because you can't put Blair in with the French.

Rumsfeld Can't I?

Powell You can't put him in with the Germans.

Rumsfeld You going to give me a reason?

This is all joshing, but now Powell raises his voice.

Powell Blair's been with us! He's been with us all along!

Cheney So?

Cheney is grinning. Now Bush joins in.

Bush Dick doesn't like him.

Cheney I don't trust him. New Labour. What the hell does that mean? We don't call ourselves the New Republicans.

Rumsfeld We're not a friggin' girl band.

Powell All right, come on, this is ridiculous. This isn't worthy of you, Dick.

Cheney Not worthy? You want me to be serious?

Powell I do.

Cheney You want me to tell you what I really think?

Powell Yes.

Cheney All right. I'll tell you. (*Cheney pauses a moment before taking aim.*) Tony Blair? I've read his stuff. I've heard him talk. This is a man on a mission. This is a man with a history.

Powell Sure.

Cheney He knows what he wants: he wants to build some new world order out of the ruins of the World Trade Center. He wants the right to go into any country anywhere and bring relief from suffering and pain wherever he finds it. And I don't. What I want is to follow this country's legitimate security concerns. And, for me, those come above everything.

Rumsfeld Me, too.

Cheney Now: if those interests happen to coincide with an Englishman's fantasy of how he's one day going to introduce some universal penalty system – three strikes and the UN says you can overthrow any regime you like – then that's fine. If not, not, and we won't miss him.

Powell That isn't fair. (*Powell shakes his head.*) Blair's loyal. He's been loyal from the start.

Cheney OK, I admit, if we want him, Blair's good at the high moral tone. If you want to go into battle with a preacher sitting on top of the tank, that's fine by me. But bear in mind, preacher's one more to carry. Needs rations, needs a latrine, just like everyone else.

Powell I like Blair.

Cheney Maybe you do. But we don't need him. And as of this moment he's bringing us nothing but trouble. (*Cheney smiles, definitive.*) It's a good rule. When the cat shit gets bigger than the cat, get rid of the cat.

Rumsfeld Nice.

Cheney This guy is putting himself halfway between American power and international diplomacy. And sorry – but that's a place where people get mashed.

Powell That's where I am, Dick. In that same place.

Cheney No. No, Colin. It's different for you.

Powell Why? Why's it different for me?

Powell waits. A real nastiness has come into the room.

Cheney Because you can come running home whenever you need.

There's a deadly silence. Nobody says anything. Rice shifts, tactful.

Rice OK. OK, we're going to wrap this up soon. Sir? Do you want to conclude?

Bush is thoughtful, seemingly immune to the atmosphere between his colleagues.

Bush Blair wants to keep on the right side of us.

Rice That's right.

Bush If he's not pro-American, he's nothing. Look at it his way round. He's staked the house. He's not going to quit. On the other hand, his government can fall. That's a real thing. It may really fall. So. (*Bush looks round.*) I'm sorry, gentlemen. We have to do what we can.

Powell gets up and stands a moment by himself.

TWENTY-ONE

The Security Council arrives. The Foreign Ministers and their Ambassadors.

An Actor On February 5th Powell is prevailed upon to make a presentation to the UN, using a sound-and-light show to demonstrate his case for the 'imminent threat'.

Powell sits down, then holds up a small vial of anthrax.

Powell My colleagues, every statement I make today is backed up by sources, solid sources.

An Actor The Head of White House Communications team, Dan Bartlett, remarks:

Bartlett We called it 'the Powell buy-in'.

Powell These are not assertions. What we are giving you are facts and conclusions based on solid intelligence.

An Actor Although Powell has spent the previous four days angrily throwing out much of the two-hundred-minute speech Cheney, the CIA and the Pentagon have given him to read, he does raise the spectre of mobile laboratories to make biological agents:

Powell The source is an eyewitness, an Iraqi chemical engineer who supervised one of these facilities.

An Actor It turns out the supposed eyewitness is actually in Germany. The CIA has never spoken to him. Hans Blix comments:

Blix I knew they'd cut a lot of stuff they claimed to have, and that left me thinking: if this is the best they've got, what on earth was the rest like?

An Actor When his turn comes, Blix offers the Council a rather different assessment.

Blix Since we have arrived in Iraq we have conducted more than four hundred inspections, covering more than three hundred sites. The inspectors have not found any weapons of mass destruction.

An Actor Later, Blix comments:

Blix I was often asked later why there was such a change in tone with my previous speech, and I used to explain that if you are asked to talk about the weather, your reports must be different when the weather changes.

Blix sits down. There is a flurry of excitement.

An Actor In the charged atmosphere Dominique de Villepin seizes his opportunity:

De Villepin War is always the sanction of failure. France has never ceased to stand upright in the face of history and before mankind. In this temple of the United Nations, we are the guardians of an ideal, the guardians of a conscience.

An Actor De Villepin turns to Colin Powell:

De Villepin This message comes to you today from an old country, France, from a continent like mine, Europe, that has known wars, occupation and barbarity. Let us give the United Nations inspectors the time they need for their mission to succeed.

An Actor As de Villepin finishes, there is an unknown noise, starting in the galleries and rippling down, a stream becoming a flood.

The sound of applause. People rise to their feet. Powell pushes away his papers.

Buoyed up by Blix's report, next day, people all over the world take to the streets.

The Council disappears.

Saturday 15th February sees the largest anti-war demonstration of all time. A hundred million protestors in six hundred cities demand the right of the inspectors to complete their work.

Blix steps out for milk.

In New York, Hans Blix goes out to get milk and finds Second and Third Avenues jammed with two hundred thousand people.

Blix I was worried I might be recognised and risk being hoisted to some demonstrator's truck as a mascot. In fact the Swedish Ambassador gave me a poster he picked up after the demonstration.

Blix shows us the poster. It says: BLIX NOT BOMBS.

It hangs on my wall now.

TWENTY-TWO

Blair's office assembles – Campbell, Manning, Jonathan Powell, etc.

An Actor On February 24th, Britain, Spain and the US table the long-awaited second resolution which will unambiguously authorise the use of force. They then begin the attempt to gather the votes they need from what come to be called 'the swinging six'.

Greenstock For weeks I was on the phones and went to endless dinners.

An Actor Jeremy Greenstock – a former Classics master at Eton – is British Ambassador to the UN:

Greenstock Cocktail parties are the best, you can get round twenty-five of the smaller countries in an hour. Your mind whirls the whole time, you have to remember all the names, the alliances, it's like a gigantic switchboard in your head. The faster you can make the connections the better, but it all needs to look effortless.

An Actor Blair embarks on a four-week marathon of whirlwind diplomacy. Baroness Amos is sent to Africa for the votes of Cameroon, Angola and Guinea. Blair calls the President of Chile, offering to make the seven-thousand-mile round-trip himself:

Blair is on the phone to Ricardo Lagos.

Blair I can come in person if you like.

Lagos I don't think that'll be necessary. (*Lagos puts down the phone.*)

An Actor A senior Whitehall figure remarks:

Senior Whitehall Figure We underestimated the dislike of the US around the world. Many small countries didn't like being pushed around. We failed to pick up the warning signs of what was a kind of peasants' revolt.

An Actor One African official:

African Official What can the Americans do to us? Are they going to bomb us? Invade us?

Greenstock I got used to hearing the Prime Minister's voice every day:

Blair How many votes will we get? Guinea? Cameroon? Angola? Mexico? Chile? Pakistan?

Greenstock I could only say, 'Four, Prime Minister: the United States, Britain, Spain and Bulgaria.' He'd say:

Blair Crumbs.

Blair goes into a TV studio.

An Actor Noting that America has promised $20.7 million and Britain £6.2 million in aid to Guinea, Trevor Macdonald asks Tony Blair:

Trevor Macdonald What is the going rate for a vote in the Security Council these days?

An Actor Blair has embarked on what he calls his 'masochism strategy' directly confronting critics of the war:

A Bereaved Mother is in the audience.

Mother I lost my only child in the World Trade Center. I can't describe to you how I will feel for the rest of my life. They killed three thousand innocent victims. How many innocent victims are you and Mr Bush going to kill? Mr Blair, don't do it. Don't do it!

Blair leaves the studio.

An Actor During the credits Blair is slow-handclapped by the audience. On his return to Downing Street, he asks his advisers:

Blair Who the fuck fixed that up? Thanks very much, guys.

There is bitter laughter in the den. Geoff Hoon is on the phone to Rumsfeld.

Hoon Donald. Donald, it's Geoff Hoon. I'm sorry to be making this call. It's not a call anyone wants to make. But I have a duty to tell you that there is a danger we may lose the next vote in Parliament. And if we do, I'm going to be unable to commit British troops in Iraq.

An Actor Rumsfeld next day gives one of his regular briefings to the press where he is asked:

Journalist Would the US go to war without Britain?

Rumsfeld To the extent they're able to participate, that would be welcome. To the extent they're not, there are workarounds and they would not be involved, at least in that phase of it.

An Actor Blair flies into a rage, calling Bush directly.

Bush with Cheney, Rice and Rumsfeld on one end, Blair with Manning, Jonathan Powell and Campbell on the other.

Blair I can't believe this! Here I am, staking my entire political existence, we're on the verge of committing British troops, I've worked – I've worked now for over eighteen months to help you on this, George, I've risked everything, I've been at your side from beginning to end, and your Secretary of Defense, George, your Secretary of Defense goes on television and says –

Bush I know. I heard. I heard what he said.

Blair He says: 'Oh don't worry, we don't need the British anyway.'

Bush Yeah, I saw that. I did see that. (*Bush looks deadpan at Cheney and Rumsfeld.*)

Blair I have to say, if you set out deliberately to destroy the coalition, I can't think of anything more disastrous and damaging.

Bush Yeah. No. Yeah, I take your point.

Blair Well?

Bush I've spoken to Donald. He says he was trying to be helpful. But he admits . . . it came out wrong.

Chirac goes into a TV studio.

An Actor But that same night it is a speech of Jacques Chirac which finally gives Blair a political lifeline.

Chirac My position is that whatever the circumstances France will vote 'No', because she considers tonight that there are no grounds for waging war.

An Actor Chirac uses the word . . .

Chirac 'Tonight' . . .

An Actor . . . to mean he is open to argument, should the situation change. But Downing Street senses an escape route at last.

The Downing Street group – Blair, Campbell, Manning – arguing flat out.

Blair Do you think we can do this?

Manning Of course we can do it.

Blair Are you sure?

Manning Look, we're defending the Alamo. This is life and death. You heard what he said.

Campbell I've got his words here.

Blair I know the words.

Campbell 'Whatever the circumstances.' France will vote no 'whatever the circumstances'.

Blair But he did say 'tonight'. That's the position *tonight*.

Campbell Of course he said 'tonight'! Of course he said 'tonight'! But he also said 'whatever the circumstances'.

The room has reached shouting pitch. Campbell is standing in disbelief.

What are you saying? Are you saying we have to play fair with the French? With the *French*? And when exactly did the fucking French play fair with us?

Downing Street dissolves.

An Actor Blair announces that attempts to pass the resolution may now have to be abandoned, not, he says, because the votes are not there, but because Chirac has rendered further diplomacy pointless. The French Ambassador in London warns David Manning:

Errera You can't really be going to use this? This is like the Soviet Union! You're deliberately distorting the President's words.

Manning Gérard, it's too good not to use.

An Actor The French Ambassador tells the BBC:

Errera We feel sorry for Tony Blair. But if it helps him to blame us for the failure of his resolution, we will not hold it against him.

Straw and Powell on phones in their separate offices.

Straw Colin.

Powell Jack.

Straw I've been asked to explain to you, the Prime Minister is facing the most difficult occasion of his life.

Powell We're following it closely.

Straw He's facing a full-scale rebellion in Parliament. Tony's asked me to make clear – he cannot survive, he has no chance of survival, he cannot even go into that debate, unless your President offers a cast-iron commitment to work for peace in the Middle East.

There is a charged silence.

Colin, I can't be clearer.

There is a silence. Bush and Powell walk out together.

An Actor Next day Bush steps into the Rose Garden –

Bush We have reached a hopeful moment for progress . . .

An Actor – and promises that he will at last publish the long-delayed road-map for Israel and Palestine.

House of Commons. Robin Cook stands.

The following day the US and the UK formally renege on their promise to seek a second resolution. The leader of the House of Commons, Robin Cook, stands up to resign.

Cook I cannot support a war without international agreement or domestic support. On Iraq, I believe that the prevailing mood of the British people is sound. They do not doubt that Saddam is a brutal dictator, but they are not persuaded that he is a clear and present danger to Britain. They want inspections to be given a chance, and they suspect they are being pushed too quickly into conflict by a US administration with an agenda of its own.

Only a year ago we and the United States were part of a coalition against terrorism that was wider and more diverse than I could ever have imagined possible. History will be astonished at the diplomatic miscalculations that led so quickly to the disintegration of that powerful coalition.

Cook is cheered as he sits.

An Actor Next day, Blair has a chance to respond when the government wins the vote for war:

Blair If this House now demands that at this moment, faced with this threat from this regime, that British troops are pulled back, that we turn away at the point of reckoning – what then? What will Saddam feel? What will the other states who tyrannise their people, the terrorists who threaten our existence, what will they take from that? Who will celebrate and who will weep?

The House of Commons disappears.

An Actor On March 20th, air-raid sirens announce the beginning of war just before dawn in Baghdad.

The sound of sirens, wailing in the distance.

TWENTY-THREE

The sirens fade.

An Actor The invasion begins. On March 27th, one week in, Paul Wolfowitz reassures Congress that Iraq will not cost a penny once it has been conquered:

Wolfowitz We're dealing with a country that can really finance its own reconstruction and relatively soon.

An Actor The military campaign is over in just forty-two days. At the end of April, President Bush does an underwater survival training course in the White House swimming pool to prepare for his tailhook landing from an S-3B Viking jet onto the aircraft carrier USS *Abraham Lincoln*, just thirty miles off the coast of San Diego.

An aircraft carrier. A huge banner saying MISSION ACCOMPLISHED.

Thanks to an artful arrangement of jump-suit groin-straps, George W. Bush, 43rd President of the United States, shows his balls to the world.

Bush gets out of his plane and struts across the deck to inspect the troops. Military bands. Parade. Then Bush speaks.

Bush We have removed an ally of Al Qaeda, and cut off a source of terrorist funding. And this much is certain. No terrorist network will gain weapons of mass destruction from inside the Iraqi regime, because that regime is no more. In these nineteen months that changed the world, our actions have been focused and deliberate and proportionate to the offence.

All of you, all in this generation of our military, have taken up the highest calling of history. And wherever you go, you carry a message of hope, a message that is ancient and ever new. In the words of the prophet Isaiah, 'To the captives, come out; and to those in darkness, be free.'

An Actor Donald Rumsfeld adds:

Rumsfeld There is, I am certain, among the Iraqi people a respect for the care and the precision that went into the bombing campaign.

An Actor Paul Wolfowitz comments:

Wolfowitz Like the people of France in the nineteen forties, they view us as their hoped-for liberator.

The aircraft carrier disappears.

An Actor One of the Americans' first actions is to disband the Iraqi army and police force, flooding several hundred thousand young men onto the unemployment market, unpaid and discontented. Meanwhile, Condoleezza Rice reveals her strategy for dealing with those countries who led opposition to US invasion:

Rice Punish France, ignore Germany and forgive Russia.

An Actor In May 2003, Paul Wolfowitz admits weapons of mass destruction had originally been chosen only for what he terms 'bureaucratic reasons':

Wolfowitz The Bush administration focused on alleged weapons of mass destruction as the primary justification for toppling Saddam Hussein by force because it was politically convenient, because it was the one reason everyone could agree on.

An Actor Blair asserts:

Blair You are just going to have to have a little bit of patience. I have absolutely no doubt at all when we present the full evidence, that evidence will be found and I have absolutely no doubt it exists because Saddam's history of weapons of mass destruction is not some invention of the British security services.

An Actor On July 23rd 2003, with the security situation worsening daily, Paul Wolfowitz explains why Americans were not greeted, as he had promised, with flowers and offers of sweets.

Wolfowitz Some important assumptions turned out to underestimate the problem.

An Actor As resistance to the occupation hardens, the counter-terrorist expert Jessica Stern observes:

Stern America has taken a country that was not a terrorist threat and turned it into one. Even if there weren't any Al Qaeda in Iraq before the Americans went in, there most certainly are now.

An Actor On September 7th 2003, the President reveals that the reconstruction of Iraq which Wolfowitz has said will be –

Wolfowitz Self-financing.

An Actor – will, in fact, cost at least:

Bush Eighty-seven billion dollars.

An Actor By September 14th, Dick Cheney is also willing to make an admission:

Interviewer Vice-President, this time last year you claimed Saddam Hussein was developing nuclear capability.

Cheney Yeah, I did misspeak. We never had any evidence that Hussein had acquired a nuclear weapon.

An Actor On October 2nd, the head of Iraqi survey group, David Kay, is asked whether, after six months, he has found any weapons of mass destruction.

Kay I've barely found lunch.

An Actor Even Colin Powell is ready to confess about the mobile biological labs which were at the centre of his UN speech:

Powell Unfortunately our multiple sourcing has turned out not to be accurate.

An Actor As to US assertions that Iraq possessed bombs, rockets, and shells for poison agents, unmanned aerial vehicles for delivering biological and chemical weapons, nuclear weapon materials, sarin, tabun, mustard agent, precursor chemicals, VX nerve agent, anthrax, aflotoxins, ricin and surface-to-surface Al Hussein missiles, not one has so far been found. One vial of Strain B Botulinum toxin is found in the domestic refrigerator of an Iraqi scientist. It is ten years old. Hans Blix comments:

Blix They wanted to come to the conclusion that there were weapons. Like the former days of the witch-hunt, they are convinced that they exist. And if you see a black cat, well, that's evidence of the witch.

An Actor When asked about going to war on falsified intelligence, the President's spokesman replies:

Fleischer The President has moved on. And I think, frankly, much of the country has moved on as well.

An Actor When asked where Osama bin Laden is, the President replies:

Bush I don't know where he is. I have no idea and I really don't care.

An Actor When asked on February 2nd 2004 by a reporter:

Reporter Do you think the country is owed an explanation about the Iraqi intelligence failure before the election so the voters have this information before they elect a new President?

An Actor The President replies:

Bush First of all I want to know all the facts.

An Actor The previous September, Colin Powell attends a lunch of *New York Times* editors.

   Powell is at a lunch with Editors.

He is asked:

Editor Do you think Americans would have supported this war if weapons of mass destruction had not been the issue?

Powell Your question is too hypothetical to answer.

An Actor An editor then asks:

Editor Would you personally have supported it?

An Actor Powell smiles and reaches out his hand.

Powell smiles and reaches out his hand.

Powell It was good to meet you.

All the Actors stand like a line of inspection on either side. In silence, Powell turns and, without turning back, leaves the play.

An Actor On June 4th 2003, George Bush, who, by then, has used the word 'evil' in 319 separate speeches since becoming President, reveals to the Palestinian Prime Minister:

Bush God told me to strike at Al Qaeda and I struck them, and then He instructed me to strike at Saddam, which I did.

Bush and Sharon appear before microphones.

An Actor On April 14th 2004, President Bush invites Ariel Sharon to the White House. He formally abandons the so-called road-map and gives Israel permission to implement a plan of its own, with no representation or right of negotiation offered to Palestinians.

Bush Good job, Prime Minister. Good job.

An Actor Tony Blair refuses to dissent from the new policy.

Bush and Sharon shake hands and leave.

Blair After the war, I did consider apologising. But I wasn't sure what I'd be apologising for. And besides, the moment has gone.

Blair looks at us a moment, then goes. Only an Actor remains.

An Actor Eighteen months after the invasion of Iraq, seventy per cent of the American electorate still believe that Saddam Hussein was directly involved in the planning of the 9/11 attacks.

TWENTY-FOUR

An Actor leaves. An Iraqi Exile comes on, alone.

Iraqi Exile I left my country twenty-seven years ago.
I longed for the fall of the dictator. In exile, I worked for
it. Then Donald Rumsfeld said, 'Stuff happens.' It seemed
to me the most racist remark I had ever heard.

A vacuum was created. Was it created deliberately?
I cannot comprehend. They came to save us, but they had
no plans.

And now the American dead are counted, their
numbers recorded, their coffins draped in flags. How
many Iraqis have died? How many civilians? No figure
is given. Our dead are uncounted.

We opposed Saddam Hussein, many of us, because he
harmed people, and anybody who harms innocent Iraqis
I feel equally passionately and strongly about, and I will
oppose them. And I will.

I mean, if there is a word, Iraq has been crucified. By
Saddam's sins, by ten years of sanctions, and then this.
Basically it's a story of a nation that failed in only one
thing. But it's a big sin. It failed to take charge of itself.
And that meant the worst person in the country took
charge. Until this nation takes charge of itself, it will
continue to suffer.

I mean, Iraqis say to me, 'Look, tell America.' I tell
them: 'You are putting your faith in the wrong person.
Don't expect America or anybody will do it for you.

'If you don't do it yourself, this is what you get.'